THE ENTREPRENEUR'S PLAYBOOK

First published in 2019.

ISBN: 978-1-86922-788-3 (Printed)
ISBN: 978-1-86922-789-0 (ePDF)

Published by KR Publishing
P O Box 3954
Randburg
2125
Republic of South Africa

Tel: (011) 706-6009
Fax: (011) 706-1127
E-mail: orders@knowres.co.za
Website: www.kr.co.za

Typesetting, layout and design: Cia Joubert, cia@knowres.co.za
Cover design: Marlene de'Lorme: marlene@knowres.co.za
Editing and proofreading: Jennifer Renton, jenniferrenton@live.co.za
Project management: Cia Joubert, cia@knowres.co.za

THE ENTREPRENEUR'S PLAYBOOK

From Rookie to Rainmaker in Seven Steps

by Sandy Van Dijk and Lesley Waterkeyn

kr
publishing

2019

Meaning of the Rainbow Colours

Our company, Over the Rainbow, has identified seven stages of business development that need to be mastered in order for the new entrepreneur to achieve sustainable business success. Our aim is to lead you through the rainbow colour spectrum, from getting to grips with business basics on the **red level**; to becoming proficient at branding, marketing and sales on the **orange and yellow levels**; comprehending finances and leadership on the **green and blue levels**; and achieving sustainable growth and being able to meaningfully contribute to the wider business community as you reach the **indigo** and **violet levels**.

Table of Contents

About the Authors

Lesley Waterkeyn

The founder and CEO of Colourworks (Colourworks has recently merged with Designers Ink in JHB to form a new national agency – CWDi.), Lesley Waterkeyn is a natural rainmaker whose generous and infectious entrepreneurial spirit uplifts and inspires others to do more than they imagined possible. Lesley has steered the transformation of Colourworks from a small print agency to a fully-integrated marketing agency specialising in strategic brand experiences. Colourworks was founded in 1998 and turns 20 this year. The company has an impressive client base and deals with blue-chip companies throughout South Africa.

A lifelong learner and active member of the world's largest peer-to-peer entrepreneurial network, Entrepreneurs' Organisation (EO), Lesley is passionate about unlocking the potential of South Africa's young people. She is also the co-founder of Over the Rainbow, a social enterprise that empowers young entrepreneurs with the knowledge, skills and connections that will enable them to succeed.

Amongst many other accolades, Lesley was an Africa's Women of Influence 2015 finalist, a 2015 Fairlady Women of the Future (South Africa) entrant, and the winner of the IWEC Award (International Women's Entrepreneur Challenge) in 2017.

Lesley is a married to Mark and has three boys, including a set of twins. She is one of four sisters, with two of her sisters working with her in her Colourworks and Over the Rainbow businesses. She is a keen runner and ran the New York marathon in 2017. She believes that staying fit and healthy are critical to ensuring she has the energy to continue to build her businesses and influence others to live their best lives.

Over the Rainbow

Over the Rainbow was launched in 2015 as a social enterprise that helps entrepreneurs find their pot of gold. Using the colours of the rainbow, we assist them at the various stages of their business growth to ensure success and sustainability.

Sandy Van Dijk

After leaving her teaching career of over 20 years, Sandy began searching for something to give her life new meaning and purpose. In 2014, while on a book writing experience, she met the bestselling authors, Janet Bray and Chris Attwood. She found that their Passion Test gave incredible value, so after training to become a Passion Test facilitator, she brought it to South Africa. Sandy's passion is empowering children and adults to connect to what lights them up, and for them to find purpose and meaning for themselves. Through helping others find their purpose and destiny, Sandy now gets to live her own purpose.

Sisters Sandy and Lesley founded their company, Over the Rainbow, as a social enterprise with a focus on start-up entrepreneurs. Sandy is the COO and was in charge of capturing and collating the content for this business book, which follows the colours of the rainbow. The book aims to inspire and empower young entrepreneurs to grow their businesses and achieve success.

Introduction

"Did you know that on average about 50% of all start-up businesses in South Africa fail within 24 months? One of the main reasons for the premature failure is that they are started as survivalist ventures. It is almost inevitable for them to fail because their owners do not have the skills, experience or resources to build a sustainable business", explains Ravi Govender, Head of Small Enterprises at Standard Bank.

Imagine if you had access to insights and resources that could facilitate you building a sustainable business and changing that statistic?

Our company, Over the Rainbow, has identified seven stages of business development that need to be mastered in order for the new entrepreneur to achieve sustainable business success. Our aim is to lead you through the rainbow colour spectrum, from getting to grips with business basics on the **red level**; to becoming proficient at branding, marketing and sales on the **orange and yellow levels**; comprehending finances and leadership on the **green and blue levels**; and achieving sustainable growth and being able to meaningfully contribute to the wider business community as you reach the **indigo** and **violet levels**.

In essence, the proverbial "pot of gold" is not just the measure of one's financial success, but the sustainable wealth that enables all of us to give back and participate positively in the on-going socio-development of our beautiful country.

In 1994, after the first fully democratic elections, Archbishop Emeritus Desmond Tutu called this country the Rainbow Nation. The name of our company goes beyond embracing South Africa as a rainbow nation, however, as it has a further personal meaning to us. After the sudden death of our mother and the questioning that followed, we were searching for reassurance and hope that she would remain a presence in our lives. This came to us in the form of rainbows, and throughout our lives, they have continued to be a source of guidance and inspiration. As a passionate educator and a dedicated entrepreneur, we wrote this book because we want to make a positive difference in the lives of young and aspiring impact players through support, guidance and mentorship.

While our country has gone through fantastic changes since 1994, the change is not yet deep enough; the rainbow colours are not yet bright enough and people are fed-up! We believe that tailored support for those who show resilience is what our country needs.

Sure, the world of our future needs dreamers who are prepared to do extraordinary things. And whilst the world of the future will always require the skills of doctors and lawyers, economic stability and sustainability rests largely on the shoulders of entrepreneurs. Technology is evolving at such a rapid rate that it is becoming cheaper and more accessible; we have the ability to access information and collaborate with people from all over the world at almost no cost. Good communicators, problem solvers, collaborators and flexible, creative thinkers who seek out opportunities – be they business plans, social movements or cultural shifts – is what the new business landscape will require. Solutions to the myriad of problems facing the world of today are going to come primarily from entrepreneurs.

Here's the truth. The moment you pursue entrepreneurship, obstacles will arise and they will test your character. Chaos is guaranteed, but in that chaos comes financial freedom, as well as the opportunity to inspire others and be the master of your own destiny. For a lot of people failure is something to be feared. We advocate using that fear as a tool to sharpen your perspective and strengthen your resolve. See failure not as the end of something, but as the beginning of something else.

The Global Entrepreneurship Monitor suggests that approximately 150 million businesses were started in 2016.[1] If each of these businesses employed one more person it would decrease unemployment substantially worldwide (according to the World Bank and the ILO, unemployment is over 200 million).[2]

By channelling your natural inclinations or talents into a business that you believe in and are committed to, and by sticking to your talents, you could earn respect for sustaining your business, make money doing what you love, and inspire others in your community.

As Albert Einstein once said: "If you always do what you always did, you will always get what you always got."

Two wolves

One evening an old Cherokee told his grandson about a battle that goes on inside people. He said: "My son the battle is between two wolves inside all of us. One is Evil – it is anger, envy, jealousy, sorrow, regret, greed, arrogance, self-pity, guilt, resentment, inferiority, lies, false pride, superiority and ego.

"The other is Good – it is joy, peace, love, hope, serenity, humility, kindness, benevolence, empathy, generosity, truth, compassion and faith."

The grandson thought about it for a minute and then asked his grandfather: "Which wolf wins?"

The old Cherokee simply replied: "The one you feed." [3]

Let's get started.

Chapter 1

Find your true north:
live the life you were meant to

Intention: *to discover your purpose*

Affirmation: *I'm stable, strong and healthy*

Chaos to clarity

We live in a very dynamic business environment, and given the changes in technology, analytics, marketing and customer expectations, there is an increasing need for teams to work together to manage these rapid changes. The importance of entrepreneurship cannot be underestimated; the role that it can play in advancing economies, initiating social change, and progressing education and research is prolific. In the most recent report published by the Global Entrepreneurship Monitor (GEM), the world's most notable study of entrepreneurship, it was observed that entrepreneurial activities continue to grow on a global level. In countries where the decision to start a business was predominantly initiated out of necessity, an increased share has now shifted to people starting businesses because of opportunity.[4]

Idea versus Opportunity

Just because you think you have a great idea doesn't necessarily mean it's a great business opportunity. In fact, a key reason most entrepreneurial ventures fail is not from a failure to develop products or services, but rather a lack of customers. It is important to understand what constitutes an idea versus an opportunity. Whilst ideas tend to prioritise product development, opportunities are focused on customer needs.

As an entrepreneur you need to ask yourself:

- What are the pains people are dealing with?

- How do I resolve them?

- What do people love?

- How could I further add to this enjoyment?

Being able to see an opportunity through the eyes of potential customers is what leads you to potentially viable business ideas. A great example of a business that failed to focus on customer needs and instead prioritised an idea was Amazon's Firephone. This 3D-enabled smartphone had several features that made it great for online shopping or for use in a retail store, however it failed dismally because the research team didn't concentrate on a specific market for the product.[5] Instead of focusing on the Firephone being adopted solely as a retail application and further developing relevant retail apps for the product, they launched it as a mass-market product. People already had smartphones – they didn't need another one! Unless the Firephone was going to focus on a very specific market with very specific needs it was destined to fail. This doesn't mean ideas are bad – ideas are powerful and necessary in the design process of your potential product or services, but they need to be developed after an opportunity has been identified.

So, what distinguishes an idea from an opportunity? Let's look at these four areas:

1. Timeliness

2. Fit

3. Real Customer Benefit

4. Accessibility

Timeliness: Timing really is everything. Entering a market too early or too late can have a significant impact on whether your business succeeds or fails. Whilst a young start-up might be inclined to enter the market as early as possible in order to beat the competition and grab onto those influential early adopters, it doesn't come without risks. With limited resources and a tight budget, entering too early can leave a young start-up reeling. Sometimes the best tactic is to approach the market with caution and learn from others' mistakes. Take for example the likes of **Google** and **Facebook**. Under no circumstances were they the first search engine and social media application, but they were very fast followers. They learnt from the likes of Yelp and Myspace and adapted their offerings accordingly.[6]

Fit: The best way to ensure you're building a valuable start-up is to ensure you leverage the skills and knowledge you already possess.

When we talk about "fit" we're referring to how your own expertise and experience as an individual relate to the opportunity at hand. While you might identify a real need and opportunity in the marketplace, it doesn't help if you don't possess the necessary skills, interest, experience and know-how. Teaming up with someone who might have the specific skills is a potential option – choose wisely and with care.

Real Customer Benefit: In identifying a potential opportunity that could manifest into a successful product or service, it's critical that you look at the value proposition. A value proposition is something that creates real customer benefit. It's important to recognise that an opportunity needs to solve a real problem or fulfil a real need!

Accessibility: The fourth way of being able to differentiate between an idea and an opportunity is to assess whether you will be able to create customer value that is accessible to other customers. Are you able to identify specific features and benefits that will ensure your product or service is appealing to a range of customers who will make the effort of pursuing this opportunity financially viable?

There are many reasons why it can be hard to stick to good habits or develop new skills.

Your mind is a powerful thing. The stories you tell yourself and the things you believe about yourself can either prevent change from happening or allow new skills to blossom.

While there isn't a fool-proof map to entrepreneurial greatness, one thing is for sure, successful entrepreneurs possess certain characteristics and traits:

- They are resilient, driven and ambitious.
- They are not afraid to take risks.
- They are innovative and able to identify opportunities where there is a business need.

- They are willing to put a significant amount of effort into making something work.

- They have strong money management.

- They are self-confident and dedicated.

Carol Dweck is a researcher at Stanford University who is well-known for her work on "the fixed mindset vs. the growth mindset". She describes the difference between these two mindsets and how they impact your performance:

> *"In a fixed mindset students believe their basic abilities, their intelligence, their talents, are just fixed traits. They have a certain amount and that's that, and then their goal becomes to look smart all the time and never look dumb. In a growth mindset students understand that their talents and abilities can be developed through effort, good teaching and persistence. They don't necessarily think everyone's the same or anyone can be Einstein, but they believe everyone can get smarter if they work at it."*[7]

The benefits of a growth mindset might seem obvious, but most of us are guilty of having a fixed mindset in certain situations. That can be dangerous because a fixed mindset can often prevent important skills development and growth, which could sabotage your health and happiness down the line. For example, if you say, "I'm not a maths person", then that belief acts as an easy excuse to avoid practicing maths. The fixed mindset prevents you from failing in the short-run, but in the long-run it hinders your ability to learn, grow, and develop new skills. Meanwhile, someone with a growth mindset would be willing to try maths problems even if they failed at first. They see failure and setbacks as an indication that they should continue developing their skills rather than a signal that indicates, *"This is something I'm not good at"*.

As a result, people who have a growth mindset are more likely to maximise their potential. They tend to learn from criticism rather than ignoring it, to overcome challenges rather than avoiding them, and to find inspiration in the success of others rather than feeling threatened. It's pretty clear that those with fixed mindsets will avoid experiences where they might feel like a failure. As a result, they don't learn as much and it's hard to get better. What can they do about this? How can they change the things they believe about themselves, eliminate their fixed mindset, and actually achieve their goals? To change the type of person that you believe that you are – to build a new and better identity for yourself – you need to do so with small, repeated actions.

I would like to share a story about my sister, Lesley, with you:

"Five years ago I decided to set myself a big hairy audacious goal (BHAG), which was to run the New York marathon. The truth is I am not built for running, but I dedicated my year to training; having a goal made all the difference. I was slow, but I could at least feel good that I was running regularly. I'd have good days where I would run easily and feel great, but I also had lots of bad days where I was tired and just didn't feel like running. In retrospect those days were almost better than the good days because they reinforced my goal – I didn't quit. I had modest aspirations and didn't really care if I was great at running. I just wanted to stick to my one goal and stay committed, which wasn't easy with two small children as well as running my own business. Slowly but surely, I started to think of myself as a runner. In November 2012, prior to leaving Cape Town, we learnt that hurricane Sandy had hit New York. As it happens, this turned out to be the deadliest and most destructive hurricane of the season and the second costliest hurricane in United States history. The newspaper reports stated that New York had survived 911 and they would survive this and hold the marathon no matter what. With that assurance, my husband and I packed our bags and off we went, only to arrive to a city of devastation. Our hotel was closed and roads were flooded, but assurances kept coming that the marathon would continue. Before going to bed that night, my husband went down to the bar to have a last drink before bed and 10 minutes later he came back to the room to inform me that the race had been cancelled. I remember sobbing uncontrollably.

"It took me a very long time, five years to be exact, to get over this disappointment, but it was time to get back on the road and revisit this unfulfilled dream. Standing on the start line of the largest marathon in the world with approximately 52,000 runners is an awe-inspiring and emotional experience. I was carried by the noise and elation through the boroughs, and by the time I was able to comprehend that I was going to achieve my goal, I was running over the Brooklyn Bridge and the euphoria was overwhelming. The finish line of the New York marathon was within my grasp and the surreal feeling of jogging through Central Park, at last, was a dream come true."

Lesley simply focused on the process. She focused on showing up. She focused on sticking to the schedule. She focused on "not quitting". Eventually, the results and the self–confidence came anyway. Her actions shifted the way that she saw herself. *"I've started to think of myself as a runner."*

Entrepreneurs who have embraced a growth mindset:

- recognise and embrace their imperfections;
- stop constantly seeking approval;
- enjoy the process as opposed to just the end result;
- develop a sense of purpose;
- are open to feedback that is both positive and negative;
- find the lesson in failure;
- celebrate the achievements of others;
- learn something new each day, no matter how small;
- acknowledge that they always have a choice; and
- choose to be positive, even if they have to fake it until they make it!

Here is some inspiration from some fellow South African entrepreneurs:

Lele Mehlomakulu is the founder of mPower People Solutions, a strategic human resources and organisational development company. She has sat on various Boards and Board Subcommittees, and is passionate about the development of people in organisations. Her particular interest is women and young professionals transitioning through various periods in their careers, as well as individuals who want to come out of their shells and achieve great things. She is South Africa's first Certified Daring Way™ Facilitator based on the research of Dr. Brené Brown. Lele is a Consultant, Facilitator, Coach, Speaker, Trainer and Organisational interventionist.[8]

Richard Rayne launched onsite training in 2001 with a R20,000 loan. It's a tech training company that sends trainers to clients' premises rather than bringing their staff to an off-site venue, which is expensive and disruptive. He was fresh out of university, having completed a BCom in information systems, and wanted to offer personalised instructor-led training that was different from generic classroom-based training. ILearn has delivered instructor-led courses to more than 60,000 people, and has sold 300 online courses since its launch. That translates into 20% year-on-year growth for the last five years. His advice to aspiring entrepreneurs? "If you don't possess a positive, never-say-die attitude, rather get a job. It's a good idea to find an experienced business coach who can guide you along a sometimes lonely journey."[9]

Nando's

Robert Brozin and Fernando Duarte were friends who went to a restaurant in Johannesburg called Chickenland. They loved the flame grilled chicken so much that they bought the restaurant and renamed it Nando – after Fernando. For years the franchise struggled until the idea of ordering at the till, sitting down and waiting for your food was born. The Nando's franchise never looked back and today they have over 1,000 stores worldwide.[10]

red & yellow
CREATIVE SCHOOL OF BUSINESS

Rob Stokes is all about seeing and seizing opportunities. In the first innings of his career he founded the digital agency Quirk and built a business, before selling to LSE-listed WPP in 2014. Today Rob spends most of his time as Chairman of The Red & Yellow Creative School of Business, which he finds incredibly fulfilling. He sits as non-exec Director on many boards and is passionate about developing, transforming and growing new and established businesses predominantly in the technology and education sectors. Rob is a pioneer and prides himself on building extraordinary teams. His passion and energy are contagious and he enjoys public speaking opportunities on topics such as the future of work, creative thinking, business strategy, innovation, digital transformation and future technology trends.[11]

CaRRoL BoYeS

Carrol Boyes started out as an English and art teacher, but her dream was always to be an artist who could earn enough money to survive from the work she produced. When she turned 35 years old, she realised that she would either have to do something practical or live with regret for the rest of her life. Fortunately for the design world, she chose to do the former.

Carrol Boyes cont.	She left her teaching post in 1990, and, ever the pragmatist, paid off her bills and debts, leaving her with enough money to survive for six months. During that time she started her fledgling business, designing products that were not only things that people needed, but which were also unique and fun to use. Today she has branded Carrol Boyes stores across South Africa, three in overseas markets including one in New York, a great online retail shop, and global stockists of her growing design range.[12]
I AM AN **ENTREPRENEUR**	A seasoned entrepreneur, deal-maker and operator of growth businesses, Andile Khumalo is the founder of I AM AN ENTREPRENEUR. This is an online and offline platform that supports and mentors younger entrepreneurs. Andile is the former Managing Director of POWER 98.7 and a former presenter of POWER Business on that station. A Chartered Accountant by profession, Andile has been an investment banker with Investec. Andile comes from a family of teachers and is passionate about education.[13]
imperial CAR RENTAL **Europcar**	Dawn Nathan-Jones' career started at the age of 21 when she joined Imperial Car Rental's co-founders, Carol Scott and Maureen Jackson. Together, the three ambitious and determined women took on other car rental giants with only five cars – and plenty of passion, grit and hard work. Her ability to continuously innovate, reinvent and drive change later landed her the coveted position of CEO of the Imperial Group's Car Rental Division, which included a number of other car rental and associate businesses.

Dawn Nathan-Jones cont.	Dawn stepped down from her role as CEO at the end of 2015, after 18 years at the helm. She was instrumental in many acquisitions and mergers, as well as the strategic repositioning of the Imperial Holdings brand in 2009. A dynamic entrepreneur and accomplished businesswoman, Dawn is passionate about contributing to the economic growth of South Africa and is a vocal advocate for the empowerment of women and young entrepreneurs; her dream is to leave a legacy of social entrepreneurship with heart. Dawn is most popularly recognised for her role as the only female 'Shark' on M-Net's Shark Tank SA, a show where entrepreneurs convince five self-made millionaires – the Sharks – to invest in their businesses.[14]
MOTHEO CONSTRUCTION GROUP GENERAL CONSTRUCTION · CIVILS · WATER · TELECOMS	Dr Thandi Ndlovu studied medicine at Fort Hare University and went to work in the Orange Farm area. She became alarmed that the health and wellbeing of the residents in the area was well below par and her clinic was filled daily with people in need of medication. She took the bold decision to change her profession and has been shattering stereotypes since opening the doors of her construction business. She is the founder and CEO of Motheo Construction and is one of SA's leading social housing developers with more than 80,000 units built.[15]

It is interesting to note that in recent years the number of female entrepreneurs in the world has been on the rise, and Africa is no exception. Women are constantly pushing the standards of their fields, breaking gender stereotypes and showing that what a man can do, a woman can also do. These bold and fearlessly ambitious female business leaders are shaping the future of the continent and inspiring countless other women to dare to dream. The impact these women entrepreneurs have highlights the contribution they make towards the growth and well-being of their societies by providing incomes for their families, employment for those in their communities, and products and services that bring added value to the world around them. They never quit and have advanced industries, disrupted markets and spurred economic growth.[16]

If being an entrepreneur is wrought with difficulties, there are three stand-out reasons why people start their own businesses:

- You may have an **idea** for a product or service that meets an unfulfilled need in the marketplace. By turning your idea into a business, you can be the first to meet that need which can result in a profitable venture. You could profit even more by teaching your idea to others.

- Those who are tired of the "9-to-5" grind leave the corporate world and enter into a more flexible **lifestyle**, which can enable them to spend more time with family and friends. A business can also appeal to those who enjoy making their own decisions without getting direction from their superiors.

- Owning your own business allows you to be more creative and express yourself. You are not restricted by having to follow a set work methodology, and you have the **freedom** to change your work processes if you wish. You can also create additional products or services to meet customer demands.

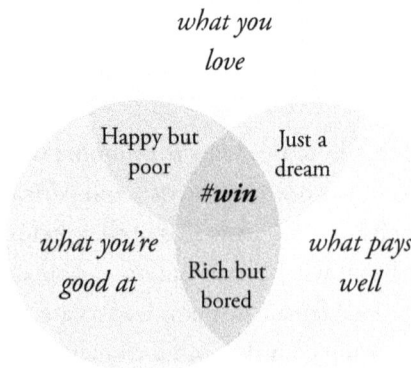

what you love

Happy but poor

Just a dream

#win

what you're good at

Rich but bored

what pays well

Figure 1: The #win situation

This diagram could help you decide what you really want if you strive towards the middle of the overlapping circles, i.e. the #win situation. Doing what you love, what you're good at and what pays well will certainly go a long way to ensuring you are not just creating a job for yourself, but a business that has value. If this is true, your new business will also make you happy, make you money, and will not just be a dream.

Here are seven steps to guide you into initiating your business journey:

1. **Clarity**

In the early stages of solving a problem that you have identified, determining the values of your operation is hugely beneficial. Values are the fundamental beliefs of an organisation; the guiding principles that dictate how people should behave and act. Although at this stage you are more than likely going it alone, the time will come when you will need to employ a team. Think about the reaction to a tense situation that you and/or your team might face in the future. Do you let your team figure it out on their own? Do you praise someone for smart improvisation? Or do you act in a way that makes people at your company nervous about making mistakes? When everyone knows what the company stands for, they'll know how to act in these moments. Those moments are the ones that keep customers coming back and ensure that your team is living authentic, reinforced core values. At Over the Rainbow, these are our values:

- **Be bold** – back yourself.
- **Be committed** – stay in it for the long run.
- **Be a lifelong learner** – constantly seek knowledge.
- **Be a leader** – gain the ability to inspire.
- **Grow and change** – make a difference in yourself, your business and your community.

It's important to remember that core values are not just buzzwords on a list that you share – they actually represent your company's core beliefs, and you don't want people on your team if they can't get behind your mission and your values. In these early stages of your business, deciding on a set of values shows your future employees, your customers and your wider community what's important to you. Values are the beliefs and guiding principles that say how people in your business behave and act.

Here are some examples of values:

Ambition	Commitment	Generosity
Communication	Empowerment	Drive
Continuous learning	Teamwork	Dedication
Creativity	Integrity	Discipline
Honesty	Predictability	Growth
Flexibility	Responsibility	Trustworthiness
Generosity	Optimism	Leadership

What values are important to your company? What traits do you want your employees to embrace? And what core set of beliefs do you want your customers to know you hold dear? In a nutshell, values describe the desired culture.

As Coca-Cola puts it, they serve as a behavioural compass. Coke's values include having the courage to shape a better future, leveraging collective genius, being real, and being accountable and committed.[17]

2. Purpose

Richard Branson is a great example of an entrepreneur. He started out selling a student magazine to cover his expenses, and despite facing many challenges and set-backs (he was dyslexic and a poor scholar), he eventually founded the Virgin Group. Today, Virgin controls more than 400 companies. Branson is one of the world's most famous entrepreneurs, and in November 2017, Forbes magazine listed his estimated net worth at $5.1 billion. While taking risks is something entrepreneurs are able to do, this story illustrates the importance of taking calculated risks.[18]

In 2004 Richard Branson started a reality show called 'The Rebel Billionaire', which was structured similarly to the Apprentice. During the final episode Richard offered the winner, Shawn Nelson, a cheque for a million dollars or an option to toss a coin for an even bigger prize. The risk was immense, as, in the end, he could get everything or nothing. He turned to Branson and asked: "OK, Richard, and what would you do?" Branson answered: "This is your own choice." Later he wrote in his book: "I could have added that I do often take a risk, but it is always a calculated risk. I invariably consider the chances, whatever the affair is."[19]

Shawn decided that he could not bet a million dollars on a coin toss. He had a small business and this money would help him to develop it and change his life for the better. Finally, after considerable thought, Shawn told Richard that he would take the cheque. Branson was very glad to hear it. "If you had decided to toss a coin I wouldn't respect you", he told Shawn. In appreciation of Shawn's calculated approach to risk taking, Richard Branson made him president of the Virgin Group for three months. In Branson's eyes, it was the right choice – Shawn did not take a risk when a situation was completely out of his control. Many see Branson as a gambler who bet big on opportunities and was lucky, but in reality, he takes calculated risks. His advice: be bold, but do not gamble; calculate the risks and take them.[20] You can reduce risk through careful planning and decision-making, and by not necessarily seeking out risks, but by anticipating opportunities.

Businesses that succeed are those that stay true to their core values and employees and customers are proud to be associated with them. Together with identifying values that you and your team can align with, you will also need a business mission and vision. Choosing the right words can send a positive ripple throughout your organisation and promote loyalty from both your team and your customers.

A mission statement is your business purpose or DOING piece. It states **who** you serve, **what** you serve them, and **how** you do it every single day. By drafting your business vision, this will help you and your future team stay focused on the activities of today that promote your dreams of tomorrow.

The vision statement is the DREAMING piece. If everything goes right, this is **how your organisation will have changed the world**. It describes where your company aspires to be in the future and should be bursting at the seams with possibility.

These two statements are often combined to clearly define the organisation's reason for existing.

Examples of mission statements:

GOOGLE – To organise the world's information and make it universally accessible and useful.[21]

PIONEER FOODS – We believe in nourishing lives with trusted, well-loved brands, empowering families to get more out of life.[22]

FLYSAFAIR – To unite people with who and what they love, by providing a low-fare, hassle-free, and on-time travel experience.[23]

VODACOM – Vodacom is a winning company where everyone is imbued with a spirit to win, to be passionate in whatever we do, to be the best, to never give up, to work harder than anybody else, to know that our best is better than anybody else's best.[24]

Examples of vision statements:

UBER – Uber is evolving the way the world moves. By seamlessly connecting riders to drivers through our apps, we make cities more accessible, opening up more possibilities for riders and more business for drivers.[25]

PetroSA – To be the leading African energy company.[26]

SPAR – To be the first-choice brands in the communities we serve.[27]

UNIVERSITY OF KZN – To be the Premier University of African Scholarship.[28]

3. Resilience

Business is a wonderful place for personal growth and learning, and it's often said that entrepreneurs are the heroes of the free enterprise economy. However, many entrepreneurs fail to become heroes for the simple reason that they plan to get rich quick, which has little to do with actually building a successful business.

Knowing how to lead, engage, develop, make decisions, take action and innovate continuously is no easy task. There will undoubtedly come a time when you will have to face some difficult conditions and situations. By building your resilience, which is being prepared for, recovering from and adapting to stress, challenge or adversity, you will be able to cope better with those tens of e-mails to be answered after a day off, the promotion that is given to your colleague and not to you, the traffic to your work, targets to be reached, etc. Without strong resilience you will be less equipped to respond properly to the situation at hand, in other words, to take responsibility. Resiliency experts say that people are helped by a particular pattern of attitudes and skills that helps them to survive and thrive under stress.[29]

> *"Simply put, these attitudes are commitment, control, and challenge. As times get tough, if you hold these attitudes, you'll believe that it is best to stay involved with the people and events around you (commitment) rather than to pull out, to keep trying to influence the outcomes in which you are involved (control) rather than to give up, and to try to discover how you can grow through the stress (challenge) rather than to bemoan your fate."* [30]

Nurturing this resilience and commitment requires the humility to confront a hundred small errors every week. The path to success is forged via a thousand small adjustments, each one possible only because, as the entrepreneur, you have your eyes and ears wide open and are able to adjust – time after time.

4. Goals

As individuals and in our organisations we are trying to improve, grow, and become more profitable. Setting goals provides the clearest way to measure success. When you are looking at your company from a three- or five-year perspective, you are looking beyond the day-to-day running of your business and instead taking a much more macro view, which allows you to see the company from a competitive, business perspective.

Setting goals ensures that everyone understands what the prize is and what they are working towards. This will eliminate a lot of the uncertainty that goes with not understanding the goals of the company. In spite of such proof of success, most people don't have **SMART** goals – **specific, measurable, attainable, realistic and time-based goals** that they work towards.[31] We would suggest that you use these guidelines to set yourself between three and five goals for the year.

- **Specific:** This is where you will give details about what you're aiming for. These goals should include answers to 'Who?', 'What?', 'Where?', 'When?' and 'Why? For example, "I would like to grow the sales and revenue of my business by 15%".

- **Measurable:** How will you know when you've succeeded and what will you use to measure the progress you've made? For example, "I will know I've reached my goal when I have completed a new website".

- **Attainable:** Your goals should be ones that you could realistically achieve. Are there additional skills or resources you will need to learn or acquire?

- **Realistic:** Make sure you can reach your goals without becoming a workaholic or a nightmare for your employees. Written statements such as, "I can achieve my goal by hiring a new employee" can be an effective motivator.

- **Time bound:** Put a deadline on your goal to help you track your progress. This stopping point ensures your success can be measured over a period of time.

Let's say that your goal is to start saving more money.

Now, in and of itself, this isn't a SMART goal, but it can easily be modified so that it becomes one.

For example:

You could say that you want to save R10,000 a year for the next ten years.

Now the goal is specific and measurable, since you have an amount that you are aiming for and the ability to measure the amount you end up actually saving. This goal is time-bound as well, since your goal is to save a specific amount each year over a given period. Whether the goal is achievable depends on your own financial situation, but assuming it is, the goal fits that criteria as well.

Lastly, you have to analyse whether saving money is a relevant and important goal for you personally. Assuming it is, then the goal in this example fits all the criteria of being a SMART goal.

Set yourself at least three written goals for your business for the year, as well as a personal goal. Information is power and the more you know, the better decisions you can make. When you set goals it's important to remember to continually monitor your business against those goals. Setting business goals doesn't guarantee the success of your organisation, but there's a lot to be said for not flying by the seat of your pants. Taking the time to look at your organisation from a broader perspective will give you greater confidence in what lies ahead and how you will be able to optimise it. We can't predict the future, but we can certainly plan for it.

In his book, *What they don't teach you in the Harvard Business School*, Mark McCormack speaks about a study conducted on students in the 1979 Harvard MBA programme. In that year the students were asked, "Have you set clear, written goals for your future and made plans to accomplish them?" [32] Only 3% of the graduates had written goals and plans; 13% had goals, but they were not in writing, and a whopping 84% had no specific goals at all.

Ten years later, the members of the class were interviewed again and the findings, while somewhat predictable, were nonetheless astonishing. The 13% of the class who had goals were earning, on average, twice as much as the 84% who had no goals at all. And what about the 3% who had clear written goals? They were earning, on average, 10 times as much as the other 97% put together.

5. Persistence

One of the main things that separate successful people from the rest is being disciplined and making smart decisions. Everything always takes longer than expected – often two to three times longer – and it can be difficult to keep things going when you're not seeing instant traction and success. Refuse to give up, turning and trying each option over and over with equal enthusiasm, knowing that eventually you will break through to a new and better way of doing things. Often we talk ourselves out of following up with a potential client and simply resort to giving up because deep down we feel that there is something about it that is wrong. As an entrepreneur, you are solving people's problems and by being persistent you trust that what you are offering is a solution to your client's problems. If you are certain that your product or service can solve your client's problem, be deaf when you are told no and try a different approach. Don't think a repetitive approach is always going to win your client over. Decide what you are going to do differently to other similar businesses. Know what you want to achieve in the long run, be persistent, trust your own judgment and stay focused.

Obstacles, challenges and yes, even failures, are guaranteed along the way; take advantage of the lessons you learn and use them as opportunities to grow. "When you lose, don't lose the lesson."[33]

6. Focus

Staying focused in this world we live in is an essential tool. You can't catch two rabbits! Fix your vision on the most important components of your business; just like a car dashboard reports car performance elements such as fuel consumption, oil level and speed, as a business leader you can monitor your 'daily dashboard' by focusing on these essentials:

- **Customers** – they are the lifeblood of a company, they provide revenue and we should be constantly aware of how they feel about our products, pricing, service, support, warranties, and the overall buying experience.

- **Solutions** – we should be driven to satisfy our customers and keep them happily buying. To this end we need to design and build products that constantly surprise and delight.

- **Money** – we need to watch revenues, margins, expenses and profits, and know how much money we have in the bank each day and which bills need to be paid and when.

- **People** – spend a portion of your day visiting valued workers to learn if they are engaged, well trained, customer focused and results driven. Recognise employees who excel and help those who need improvement.

If we look at big companies like Red Bull, Google, Tashas and Toyota, all these successful endeavours had a determined entrepreneur at the helm who formulated a clear, yet ambitious and sometimes impossible, vision behind their success. Take Colonel Sanders, for example. In 1930, the then 40-year-old Sanders was operating a service station in Corbin, Kentucky, and it was there that he began cooking for hungry travellers who stopped in to fill up. He didn't have a restaurant yet, so customers ate at his own dining room table in the filling station's humble living quarters. In 1952, at the age of 62, Colonel Sanders franchised his "Kentucky Fried Chicken" for the first time. Today, KFC has over 18,800 outlets in 118 different countries and territories around the world.[34]

Successful entrepreneurs have a common way of upholding their vision. On the one hand, they remain engaged to the extreme, and on the other, they surround themselves with great people who helped them turn their dream into a reality.

7. Never give up

The success of a venture is not only about defining and pursuing a vision, but also about creating something tangible and then being able to share it. This last part is critical as you will need to be able to instil the same passion, energy, dedication and drive to a wider audience and team. When the vision gets spread across the organisation, it translates into culture. We'll talk more about this in the Leadership/Blue chapter.

Before he became famous, Jim Carrey was trying desperately to make it in Hollywood. In 1990 he was living in his beat-up old Toyota and would drive to the Hollywood Hills overlooking Los Angeles and contemplate and visualise success. To make himself feel better he wrote himself a cheque for $10 million for "acting services rendered", post-dated it to Thanksgiving

1995, and put it in his wallet. The cheque remained there until it had almost deteriorated. When Carrey was cast in Dumb and Dumber in 1995, he was paid $10 million. We challenge you to write yourself a cheque and post-date it. When you focus your full attention on that which you choose to create in your life, it will begin to show up. Love what you do, the results will take care of themselves.[35]

One of the most powerful mind exercises you can do is visualisation. We've tried and tested it and know that it works. Olympic athletes have been using it for decades to improve their performance. The best way to use this visualisation process is to create a vision board. Your vision board will help you identify those things you want to show up in your life and give you clarity.

You'll need:

- any kind of board/paper, or you could use a mirror;

- scissors, tape, pins, and/or a glue stick to put your board together;

- magazines that you can cut images and quotes from; and

- most importantly, the stuff you want to look at every day: photos, quotes, sayings, images of places you want to go, reminders of events, places or people, postcards from friends, and just about anything that will inspire you.

Give yourself a stress-free hour to put your board together.

Put your board somewhere where you can see it every day. This will reinforce your goals and help to keep you focused on the things you really want in your life. Now it's up to you to take action on those goals. Your conscience governs the actions you take, while your sub-conscience governs your belief system. Underpinning this is your creative sub-conscience which is your sanity and paints the picture of what you truly desire. Hence the power of creating a vision board.

Chapter 2

Build your promise:
*create credibility, trust and loyalty
within your brand*

Intention: *to feel connected to my customers*

Affirmation: *I am creative and trustworthy*

Marketing and Branding

Going back to very early commercial endeavours, businesses have worked tirelessly to make their products stand out from their competitors. Whether it was having the highest quality product, creating an emotional link with customers, or undercutting prices, companies have consistently strived to use a wide range of tactics to promote themselves. These tactics are what we refer to as marketing. Marketing is the sum total of specific activities and strategies a business embarks on to encourage people and other businesses to buy (and continue buying) its products and services. Every business benefits from marketing; they just need to figure out what mix of approaches and tactics suit them, their budget and the offering they have for their customers. Marketing's aim is to connect with the outside world and to get to know and understand your customer so well that your product or service fits him or her and sells itself.

Marketing is born out of psychology and economics – we buy with our hearts before our heads.

Having a conversation with your potential customers is vitally important so that you understand their hopes and dreams. It's from them that you get ideas which could be turned into products or services. It is important to understand a key difference here: "forming a relationship" happens every time a person connects with your company, and "building a relationship" takes place through repeated conversations. It's these repeated conversations that will build lasting relationships.

Clay Christensen, renowned Harvard Business School Professor and author of the bestselling book, *The Innovator's Dilemma*, believes that in order for business, and indeed start-ups, to be successful, they need to stop selling products and services to customers based on market segmentation. Instead they should focus on trying to help people address their jobs-to-be-done.[36]

Traditionally, companies tend to plan and launch new products or services based on segmenting their market and then positioning the merchandise or service accordingly. Segmenting a market might involve dividing the market based on product categories (either function- or price-based) or dividing customers according to specific demographics (age, gender, education etc.) Whilst these practices can work, they're not always reliable, and with 95% of new product launches failing each year, Christensen believes there's a different way to approach this challenge.

So what do we mean when we talk about jobs-to-be-done?

The theory around jobs-to-be-done focuses on what items, products or services consumers 'hire' to get a specific task done. Adopting a jobs-to-be-done perspective requires businesses to crawl into the skin of their customer and focus on how they go about their day, constantly asking the question: "Why did they do it that way?"

It's perhaps easier to think about the word 'job' as being shorthand for what a specific individual is really looking for to accomplish something in a given circumstance. As an entrepreneur it's your responsibility to understand what job your customer is trying to fulfil, and then design a product with associated experiences and uses to do that job. You then need to focus on delivering that product or service and selling it in a way that reinforces its intended role, so that customers find themselves choosing your product or service over anything and everyone else.

Milkshake Marketing

To give further insight into how the jobs-to-be-done theory works, Christensen gave an example a client of his had around milkshake sales:

A well-known fast food chain was having trouble increasing their sales for milkshakes. Did they need to make them more chocolatey, fruitier, thinner or thicker? The company had followed the traditional route of segmenting their market according to their product (the milkshakes) and by demographics (the profile of a typical milkshake drinker). The company then asked people who suited their pre-defined demographic to name all the characteristics of their ideal milkshake. The answers came back: chocolatey, fruity, thin, thick, smooth, etc. The chain's marketing division responded to the feedback and yet their milkshake sales still didn't improve.

Enlisting the help of one of Christensen's researchers, the fast food company approached the challenge by trying to understand what 'job' the customers were 'hiring' the milkshake to get done. Christensen's researcher spent a full day at one of the fast food chain's outlets reviewing and documenting everyone who bought a milkshake; when did they buy them, who bought them, what time did they buy them, and did they drink them on the premises?

The results of the researcher's observations showed that a whopping 40% of milkshakes were bought first thing in the morning by commuters who ordered them to go. But why? The next morning the researcher went back to the fast food outlet and started to interview the customers who left with a milkshake in hand. He asked them what job they had hired that milkshake to do.

At first they were a little perplexed, however after probing further as to why they ordered the milkshake instead of something else, most of the customers replied with the very same answer. They had hired the milkshake because they had a long commute to work and needed something to take up that time and make the journey less monotonous. Furthermore, they knew that they needed something of sustenance to keep them full until lunch at 12:00, and it had to be something they could have whilst driving. They could have just as easily 'hired' a bagel to do the job or a piece of toast, but the customers pointed out that both would be too messy; a piece of fruit also could be 'hired' to do the job but it would be eaten in a few bites. The customers explained that by 'hiring' the milkshake they had something delicious to drink, it lasted a long time thanks to the thick consistency and the thin straw, and they only needed one hand to drink it.

By understanding the job that needed to be done, the fast food company was able to respond by developing a series of morning milkshakes that were even thicker to last the long commute, and had a range of flavours and textures such as the addition of chunks of fruit. They were also able to identify a separate job that customers required milkshakes for! Parents often wanted to give their children a treat after school or a sports match but didn't want to wait forever for them to drink it, so the restaurant responded by creating a milkshake with a thinner consistency that was equally delicious but could be sucked up through a straw in a much shorter amount of time![37]

When following this method, it's important to keep in mind that a "job" is not a description of what the customer is doing or the steps they are taking to get a job done. Instead, the "job" expresses what the customer is ultimately trying to accomplish.

A deep understanding of the specific job that needs to be done will enable businesses to apply innovative product development and marketing efforts without guessing what trade-offs their customers might be willing to make.

We've listed four principles below that support the jobs-to-be-done approach:

- People buy products and services to get a "job" done.

- Jobs can be functional, emotional or social.

- Having a deep understanding of the customer's "job" makes marketing more effective and innovation far more predictable.

- People look for products and services that allow them to get an entire job done on a single platform.

Here are seven steps to consider as you endeavour to solve your customers' problem, design your brand and get your message to the market.

1. Understand your product or service

In short, a person's perception is his or her reality. You may have a product or service that could satisfy the needs of the members of a particular market segment, but your customers don't know that yet. So, you have the challenge of figuring out how to persuade them to buy from you. Let's start by asking these questions:

- What is the purpose of your product or service for the customer?

- How can your customers access it; how is it delivered to them?

- How much does it cost?

- How economical or sustainable is it to produce?

- What are the wider implications of using your product, environmentally or socially?

All of this information should be communicated both verbally and in written form – on the back story of your product, on the pages of your website, or within your product literature or brochures. Your staff and salespeople will need to be able to deliver this information and must be able to explain it in a simplified, customer-centric way. In the end, getting your product or service noticed involves influencing the perceptions of others. If you are going to build a successful business you need to sell value – value is not what you get it's what you give.

2. Know your audience

You need to create a human connection with your potential customer. Think of something that you know absolutely *everybody* likes. What came to mind? Holidays? Well, time off actually stresses some people out more than it relaxes them. Puppies? Some people are afraid of or allergic to dogs. Chocolate? As strange as it might seem, not everybody loves chocolate. It's hard to think of something. People are all different – we all like, want and need different things. Our choices are motivated by our personal thoughts and preferences. Your business works the same way. It's not a "one size fits all" solution. There are certain people who will absolutely love your product or service and rave about it until the cows come home. Others simply won't see the point or value in what you're offering. It's for this very reason that it's so important to identify your ideal customer.

Understanding who they are, where they live, what their income bracket is, and what their exact needs are will help you craft your marketing message. This information helps you determine their specific needs and how to meet them. Your product or service must solve a problem and add value to their life or work. Creating a strategy with your ideal customers in mind will help you avoid wasting time and resources on unsuccessful marketing efforts, and by listening to your customers' needs you can put your resources to work in powerful and profitable ways. Take a look at the diagram below. The big question is: "What problem are you solving for your ideal customer?" This customer should share your same world view, have the time and the money to spend, understand what your business is about, and become familiar with your product or service. All of these factors will affect the way you engage with them in meaningful and useful ways.

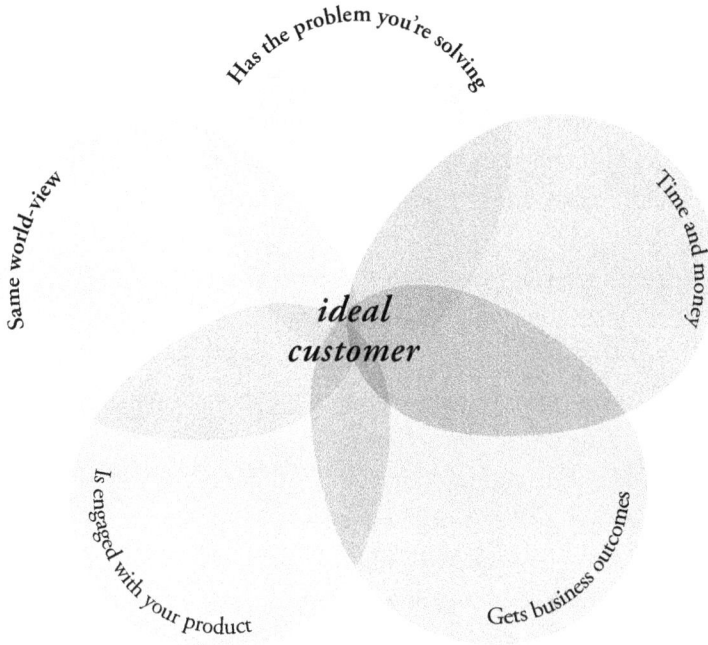

Figure 2: Identify your ideal customer

3. **Identify your competitors**

All businesses face competition. Even if you're the only restaurant in town you must compete with movie houses, bars and other businesses where your customers will spend their money instead of with you. So knowing who your competitors are and what they are offering can help you to make your products, services and marketing stand out. It will enable you to set your prices competitively and help you to respond to rival marketing campaigns with your own initiatives. Find out as much as possible about your competitors. Read about them, go online, speak to them and then evaluate the information you find. This should tell you whether there are gaps in the market that you can exploit. Ask yourself:

- What can I learn from my competitors and can I do better?

- What are they doing worse than us?

- What are they doing the same as us?

Once you have done your research on who your current or potential competitors are, then you have to assess their strengths (e.g. customer base, revenue base, cash resources and product offering) and weaknesses to see if you can build a better customer experience within your budget.

4. Marketing strategy

Your marketing strategy should be to motivate your customer to buy your product. In the process of understanding what your customer needs and how best to satisfy those needs, you will be creating a demand for a product or service. It's also understanding what your USP, or unique selling point, is – be it economy, service, quality, price, uniqueness, anything. Are your customers identifying with the personality of your company? And most importantly, are you making a difference to their lives? Here are some suggestions:

- What physical act do I want people to take after being exposed to my marketing (click here, call a phone number, complete this coupon, or look for my product next time they're at the store)?

- What prime benefit do I offer?

- What competitive advantage do I want to stress?

- What marketing weapons will I use?

- My marketing budget will be _____% of our projected gross sales.

Tell everyone about the new product or service and get publicity for your new offering. Decide which media outlet will have the sort of readers who would want to buy your new product or service. A well-worded email gives your business credibility and allows you to make direct contact with your customer. You can promote specials and drive traffic to your website. Your business website is a salesperson that never sleeps, working to promote your company and sell your products 24/7, and can be visited from anywhere in the world. Whether you sell your products online or just use the website to establish a sense of legitimacy, it should contain the right key words for your industry so that when people search for you online, they can find you. We call these key words search engine optimisation, or SEO. Your email list and free membership is the perfect strategic tool to listen to what your ideal audience is saying in terms of frustrations and challenges. As you get your audience engaged and sharing, you then begin building products and services to meet those wants, needs, and desires. This is the hidden value of having a dedicated community around your brand.

The diagram below shows how to create brand awareness by using an effective digital marketing strategy. Social media is an affordable way to keep your customers up-to-date and interested, and your brand top-of-mind. Choose just three channels and analyse your findings from these campaigns so you can measure where your customers choose to engage with you and how to build your customer relationships.

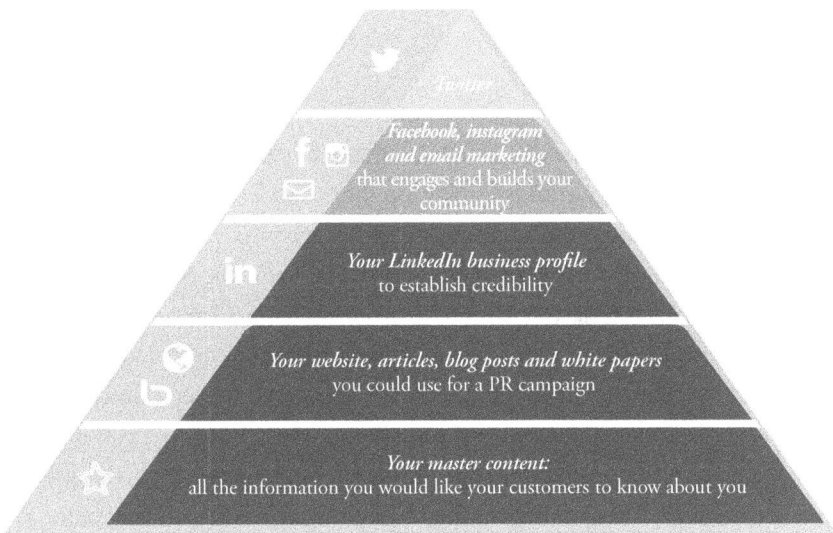

Twitter

Facebook, instagram and email marketing that engages and builds your community

Your LinkedIn business profile to establish credibility

Your website, articles, blog posts and white papers you could use for a PR campaign

Your master content: all the information you would like your customers to know about you

Figure 3: Digital marketing strategy

Before embarking on a specific marketing strategy, it's important for a business to review any internal or external factors that might impact or influence its marketing efforts. A great way to do this is via a SWOT analysis. Essentially, a SWOT enables a business to:

- highlight its **S**trengths;

- acknowledge its **W**eaknesses;

- identify **O**pportunities to build on; and

- target **T**hreats to reduce or eliminate.

Strengths	How do I use these to my best advantage?
Weaknesses	How do I work around them?
Opportunities	What actions do I need to take advantage of them?
Threats	What steps must I take to avoid them?

When conducting a SWOT analysis it's helpful to keep the following tips in mind:

A SWOT analysis is subjective, not scientific. Aside from yourself, try and get other people in your team to help develop the SWOT analysis (for additional input) and be prepared to rework your analysis every six months or so. Have a specific timeframe in mind by making sure you focus the SWOT on what your business is like today, where you want to get to in 12 months, and how you'll get there. Be real and be honest. Whilst there is no need to downplay your strengths, there's equally no reason you should be overemphasising them either. In order to get the best out of your SWOT analysis you need to be realistic and honest about your business and environment. Think of your competitors. What is the competition doing and how are they better or worse than you? How might these issues play into your marketing strategy? Keep the process simple! A SWOT analysis is still just a tool – it's not your marketing strategy. Develop your SWOT properly but don't overthink it; move on to the real deal which is developing your marketing strategy.

5. Deliver your message clearly

In an increasingly competitive marketplace, brands have to strive for differentiation, promote growth and relevance, and have a clear purpose for the customer. Purpose is central to a brand, its identity and the business that brought it to life. In order to understand the purpose of a brand, and indeed a business, one needs to ask: "Why?" Aside from making a profit, why does your brand exist? The best place to start when attempting to work out the 'why' of your brand is to review Simon Sinek's work. He talks about the 'why' of a brand through the lens of a Golden Circle.

The Golden Circle

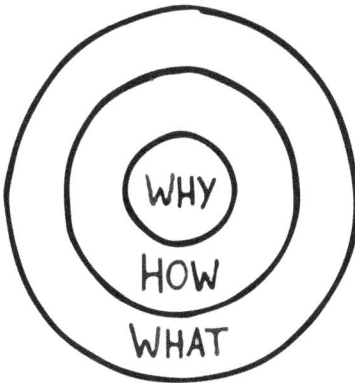

What
Every organisation on the planet knows WHAT they do. These are the products they sell or the services they offer.

How
Some organisations know HOW they do it. These are the things that make them special or set them apart from their competition.

Why
Very few organisations know WHY they do what they do. WHY is not about making money. That's a result. It's a purpose, cause or belief. It's the very reason your organisation exists.

Figure 4: The golden circle[38]

Understanding the deeper 'why' a business and its brand exists provides a sturdy foundation upon which everything else –the 'how' (brand experience, organisational culture) and 'what' (what products or services you offer) – can be built.

35

Whilst the role of brands used to be restricted to providing consumers with a sense of belonging, they now allow individuals to make friendships (Facebook), create knowledge (Wikipedia), share and generate films (YouTube) and create a market place (eBay or Bid or Buy). The power of brands is incredible, and as Meg Whitman, the former CEO of HP, once said, "When people use your brand as a verb, that is remarkable!"[39] Think about how we use the term "Google it" to mean searching for something online, "Instagram it" as a reference to taking a photo and posting it on social media, or "I'll Skype you" as an indication that we will call someone.

Whilst brands traditionally used to belong to farmers, manufacturers, advertisers and multinational organisations, today brands belong to each of us. Every day people either make or break brands through the use of them – they now mean what you say they mean.

Everything from your logo to your website, your social media experiences, the way you answer the phone, and the way your customers experience your staff needs to be part of a well thought-out, strategic plan. People tend to do business with companies they are familiar with. If your branding is consistent and easy to recognise, it can help people feel more comfortable when buying your products or services. We wear brands, eat brands, listen to brands, and are constantly telling others about the brands we love. Ultimately, your brand is the call to action for your business. On the flip side, you can't tell someone about a brand you can't remember. A strong brand is critical to getting those referrals, building your network, and separating you from your competition.

The best branding is built on a strong idea and goes way beyond just a logo and a design; it's an idea that you and your staff can hold on to, commit to, and deliver upon. Your brand needs to seep into your entire business. When your business is clear on the brand and can deliver on the promise of the brand, you will gain loyalty from your customers. Think of how we instantly recognise the golden arches of McDonalds, or the simple but powerful tick of Nike. As the "face" of a company, logo design is critical because that simple graphic will be on every piece of correspondence and advertising. A professional logo design is simple enough to be memorable, but powerful enough to give the desired impression of your company. If your brand is consistent and clear, it puts the customer at ease because they know exactly what to expect every time they connect with your brand.

A clear brand strategy helps you stay focused on your mission and vision as a business, and can help guide your marketing efforts, saving you time and money. Having a strong brand helps people feel good on an emotional level when they engage with your company. Everybody feels before they think, so how do we choose which brands to notice? We focus on what we already know and can relate to. When a brand makes us feel something, we carry it with us. We tell our family and friends, and we share it on our social networks. It makes us feel like we are part of something; something that we can be excited about. So give your customers what they want – a connection that is both meaningful and memorable.

According to research undertaken by Concerto Marketing, when people trust your brand:

- 83% will recommend it;

- 82% will use its products and services frequently; and

- 50% will pay more for its products and services.[40]

Brands like Coca-Cola, Apple, Ford, KFC and McDonalds have spent millions on ensuring that their brand is worth much more than all their physical assets put together.

6. Stand out

In our digitally obsessed world, you've got a lot of competition for your buyers' attention in your quest to advertise your company, service or product. Most of us are bombarded with a tsunami of commercials, adverts, brand labels, ads on your phone – anything to get your attention and compel you to buy. It's easy to stand up, but it's hard to stand out. In order to be heard above the noise you will need to be creative, memorable and engaging.

Colour schemes are more important than you might think. Different colours have the ability to stir up emotional responses, such as calm, happiness, or frustration. When it comes to using colours in your brand design, it's essential to consider your company's ideal customer. What colours will your customer respond to? Is your colour scheme overwhelming or pleasing to look at? Are you trying to convey your brand's voice with a bright and funky orange, or a professional, calming blue? Regardless of your choice, spend time researching the best colour options to leave your customers with a good impression. After all, the colours you use to advertise your business influence the buying decisions of your clients.

Here is a brief explanation of colours and their meanings in business:

- **Red** gives people the signal to act. When using red in business, use it as an accent colour to tempt buyers to buy on impulse. A touch of red to a website can help portray the business as energy-driven and exciting. Examples of companies that have used red successfully are Coca-Cola, Vodacom and KFC.

- Using **orange** in business suggests adventure, fun and travel. It is a beneficial colour for hotels, travel companies and resorts, and can stimulate social communication. Orange is friendlier and less aggressive than red. Companies that have used orange successfully are Fanta and Mango Airlines.

- **Yellow** can be used to promote point of sale purchases, especially when you want to get your customers' attention quickly. Many fast food companies are known to use red and yellow, as red encourages people to eat more, whereas yellow encourages them to move quickly. McDonalds, Shell and the iconic Veuve Clicquot champagne have used yellow successfully.

- **Green** represents nature, prosperity and money. It is especially recommended for health and healing. Dark green is a good colour for financial websites, while lime green may be used to create a buzz about products on sale or an upcoming offer. Companies like Land Rover, Animal Planet and Starbucks use green.

- **Blue** represents stability and depth. Most conservative corporate businesses have blue in some form or other in their logos, business cards and brochures. Similarly, businesses involved in communication, hi-tech, computers, water, filtration, swimming pools etc. always use blue. Examples of this are companies such as Standard Bank, Facebook and Intel.

- **Purple** is a sign of wealth, wisdom, royalty, creativity and magic. It is highly recommended for women's and children's products, while many men's products are slowly getting attuned to this colour as well. Cadbury is known for its purple colouring.

- The colour **white** in business usually represents cleanliness and hygiene. It indicates calm, simplicity and organisation. On the negative side, it can also mean coldness, detachment, sterility and disinterest. Many businesses use white as the background for their websites.

- **Black** means luxury, elegance and sophistication, and is used for selling and marketing to youth audiences. The music industry also likes to use it to portray style and trendiness. Companies that use black include Uber, Nike, Sony and Disney.

- **Pink** is the perfect colour for feminine industries. Charities also like to use pink as it evokes compassion and warmth. Victoria Secret uses pink.

- **Silver** is sleek, smooth and futuristic. It is apt for businesses that deal in computers and technology. Silver, like gold, is associated with wealth and luxury. Companies such as Apple, Honda and Lexus have used silver.

7. Create business credibility

Start by demonstrating empathy for the people on your team and your customers.

Without a doubt, your staff and stakeholders will want transparency about your business and your goals, so be honest and sincere. Transparency builds trust and enables people to feel more comfortable spending their money on, or investing in, your business.

Focus your energy and resources on only those tasks and assets that help meet your goals. By proving you have the necessary skills to accomplish those goals, you will instil confidence in your team and put your stakeholders at ease. Be proud of your achievements and allow them to speak to your credibility by sharing them on appropriate social media platforms. Be bold about asking for endorsements and testimonials from other successful professionals, especially if your role in the relationship added value and had a positive impact. If you are just starting out in your career you probably lack the achievements necessary to build credibility, but even without these, confidence is a trait that, when properly mastered, can speak volumes about you. While turning a profit is your ultimate goal, it is important to be as helpful as possible while starting and running any business. Go out of your way to help all of your customers, and invest time and effort (especially in the beginning) into providing as many resources as you can to help them. Sometimes this means creating and giving away lots of free stuff or content in order to build trust with your customers and get them to believe in your company, and ultimately do business with you over and over again. Being an entrepreneur who gets things done, stays true to his or her word and has a history of successes creates credibility "currency" that can be cashed in instantly.

Here's a story that illustrates what we mean when we say the "experience" factor of your brand.

A pitch for a marketing campaign

Saatchi and Saatchi is a global advertising agency that has a rich history of building successful brands. Legend has it that one of reasons Saatchi and Saatchi won the British Rail account was the way they treated their potential client. During the pitch process Saatchi and Saatchi invited the big wigs of British Rail to a special presentation at their offices. Saatchi kept them waiting in their shabby reception area and served them cold tea. As they waited, messages kept arriving, informing them that the CEO and his team would be there any minute.

Finally, after waiting over an hour, the British Rail executives furiously told the receptionist that Saatchi would never, ever be working for British Rail. At that very moment, the Saatchi team emerged and declared: "Well now you know how your customers feel – let's see what we can do to fix it!"

Not only did they get the business, but they created one of the world's best positioners for a transport company desperately trying to change: "British Rail. We're getting there."

Chapter 3

Commit to action:
back yourself and do whatever it takes

Intention: *to act with confidence*

Affirmation: *I can do anything I set my mind to*

Sales

The word 'sell' literally means 'to give'. You are figuring out your customers' pain and offering them a solution.

Establishing a start-up, developing a product or service, and working on a specific sales cycle to generate sales and keep your business afloat is hugely stressful. Regardless of whether you have a sales background or not, start-up founders will always find themselves stretched thin. That being said, if you can work through the early stages of figuring out a sales process that works, then you're halfway to resolving the pains that go with selling. Put simply, a sales process follows a series of predictable phases or events that you, as an entrepreneur, need to action in order to turn prospective clients into paying customers.

Have you ever heard Mark Twain's theory about eating a frog? He argued that: "If it's your job to eat a frog, it's best to do it first thing in the morning. And if it's your job to eat two frogs, it's best to eat the biggest one first."[41]

As entrepreneurs we often avoid making sales calls because of a fear of rejection. Take courage from this saying. If the first thing you do in the morning is eat a live frog, you can go through the rest of the day knowing the worst is behind you. Your frog is your worst task and should be done first thing in the morning. If you have two frogs, eat the bigger one first so that the second one won't seem quite as bad. You'll feel an enormous sense of achievement and empowerment if you adopt this strategy. Don't procrastinate; get the worst tasks out of the way so that the rest of your day runs smoothly. The truth is that behind every successful product is a killer sales pitch. Great ideas are a dime a dozen, but, as some of the world's most successful entrepreneurs know, it takes the hustle and grind of sales to build a business. Here are the stories of two successful billionaires who started out as salesmen.

Billionaire Nick Woodman is the founder of GoPro, the adventure-proof 35-millimeter camera. While on a trip in Australia and Indonesia, he put together an early prototype consisting of a waterproof camera tied to a band to record himself surfing. This is how, thanks to his mom's sewing machine and a few hundred dollars, GoPro was born.

Woodman and his wife sold shell necklaces they bought for $1.90 in Bali along the California coast for $60 each. While the necklaces may have seemed small and insignificant, Woodman noticed that this jewellery served as more than decoration – it represented a beach-bum, adventurous lifestyle that people were willing to pay for.

His sales secret: Sell the lifestyle

"GoPro is all about celebrating an active lifestyle and sharing that with other people. It's authentic. It's not a brand that we went out and bought a bunch of ads for to create."

Just like with his necklaces, Woodman decided to sell the lifestyle associated with the product, rather than the product itself. His entire marketing campaign is centred on the jaw-dropping experiences of people using a GoPro. Woodman sells the stories, the adventures, and the lifestyles that GoPro will capture – aided by the high-quality footage his product produces.[42]

John Paul DeJoria is best known as the co-founder of John Paul Mitchell Systems, hair products that stock the shelves of over 150,000 salons worldwide.

When DeJoria started John Paul Mitchell Systems, he sold the products out of the boot of his car. For two years he barely made rent while the company was on the verge of bankruptcy. Yet because he was able to stomach rejection for two straight years, his business was still standing when he finally caught his big break. This resilience and grit is what enabled him to grow John Paul Mitchell Systems into a multi-million dollar business.

His sales secret: Survive the no

DeJoria always says that what separates successful people from unsuccessful people is that successful people do the work that no one else wants to. Part of that is having the persistence to keep trying, no matter how many people shoot you down.

"I don't care how good your idea is, no matter how unique it is, you're going to get a lot of rejection. You have to be able to knock on door number 100 and be just as enthusiastic at that door as you were on the first 100 doors that were slammed in your face."[43]

Now that you've created interest, how are you going to turn your marketing efforts into sales? Because at the end of the day – sales solve everything! Think of the sales process in terms of riding a bike up a hill. When you start peddling you have to gain momentum to get the bike going and this takes a lot of energy. Once you've been riding for a while, however, you develop a flow; you can even free wheel at times. As you ride you build up steam, so when you hit a hill, it's easier to climb because you have momentum.

That's what an effective sales process is like. Starting out takes extra energy as you put your plan in place, but once you get going, it becomes easier to maintain. You still have to pay attention to what you're doing, but sticking with it and realising results becomes easier the more you pedal. However, if you start and stop, and start and stop, you'll be exhausted and have nothing to show for it. You aren't going to do business with everyone. And even if you were, you have to start somewhere; you have to focus somewhere in order to build up that momentum we talked about. First, create a list of potential customers. It should be large enough to give you the opportunity to really delve in and repeat the process a couple of times. If your target market is too small, your odds of success decrease. You may have to merge two similar target markets in order to make the numbers work in your favour.

Once you've created your list, reach out to your networks to see if you're connected in any way to the person or organisation you're seeking. The value of your network can end up contributing to your net worth. You're looking for an introduction – an opportunity to meet with a potential client. When your friend or associate introduces you, follow up and set up a meeting. This includes calling, emailing and exploring contacts. When you're invited to a function, have an elevator pitch at your fingertips. This is an ice breaker; a description of yourself and what your company has to offer in a nutshell. When you meet people, you typically have just 60 seconds to leave an exciting, impactful and meaningful impression. This succinct sentence should answer why you are in business. Make your pitch about the solution your business has come up with and how you are proposing to help your prospective client solve a problem. Make it count.

Having too many options can get confusing. We suggest starting with five to six target companies to focus on. Once you've made some progress with those five or six, you can expand your search.

Here are seven sales techniques to consider as you embark on your sales strategy:

1. Value first, price second

Perhaps the key to any sales process is communication. When you're selling a product or service, the way you communicate is crucial – regardless of whether it's face-to-face, over the phone, or via email. People tend to make up their minds about the rest of the conversation (and you) within the first few seconds of meeting. This decision is based on your tone, manner and even the inflection of your voice. You might be able to change their impression at a later stage, but it's a lot easier to make a positive impression the first time around. One of the cardinal rules of sales is to only start discussing price once your prospective customer fully understands the value of your product or service. Research indicates that people use cost as a gauge for quality. By bringing up cost too early in a conversation, a prospective buyer might believe your product/service is too expensive and out of their reach OR too cheap to do the job.

If you understand your product's features this allows you to present its benefits accurately and persuasively, and your customers will respond to your enthusiasm. Customers are more inclined to trust salespeople who show confidence in themselves and what they are selling. You can build this confidence by increasing your knowledge of your product or service, drawing on your own experience of using it, listening to feedback from your customers, visiting the manufacturer, and being aware of what your competitors are up to. The first step is to get them to try your offering, which can be a difficult task. Here are some tips to help you:

- Lay out your argument in terms that are as clear and concise as possible. For example, "Our new cookies taste the same as the one you are currently eating, but they have 50% fewer calories and contain no fat". Clearly, taste is a matter of personal opinion, but a lower calorie content and no fat are facts that will convince at least some people that your product is a healthy alternative that is worth trying.

- Try to use demonstrations that highlight the value of your offering, especially if the benefits are visible, e.g. for weight loss, before and after photos may be useful. Presenting the results of tests you have conducted can change people's opinions, especially if these tests have been done by a third party.

- There are people who are always willing to try new things. If you provide incentives, offer free samples and satisfy these customers, they will be more likely to purchase your product or service in the future.

- If the right people are seen using your product or service, others may be persuaded to give it a try. For example, Nike will often sponsor equipment to high-visibility athletes or teams. The athletes who wear the running shoes are "influencers" and will prompt others to purchase this or another Nike product.

- Try to get endorsements from prominent/influential people. Think of authors; they often get experts in their field to write on the back cover of their books, and that way people who respect the opinions of the experts will buy the books.

As you engage with your customers, you can use your knowledge to lead them through the sales process and make their experience an enjoyable one that they'll want to revisit.

2. **Sell the solution, not the product**

We keep on coming back to this point, but it's crucial. In order to optimise sales and drive growth for your start-up, you need to focus on the pains and gains you're solving for your potential customer. Selling a solution leads to trust, and, over time, a dedicated customer following.

You now have the opportunity to meet your potential customer in person. This is your golden time to make sure you understand what success looks like for them. It's time to deliver on what you said you were going to do and begin to build a relationship. In the beginning this could mean listening with your full focus to what your new client's struggles are, and there may be a hidden agenda. Try to see things from your customer's perspective; really listen to what is going on in their world. How are you going to be of service to your new customer? Make sure you're very clear about the problem you're trying to solve. If you have an expectation exchange you will be able to take your new client from their pain point to a promise. Get to know them, their needs, and their business practices. By understanding their business, the personalities involved and their buying motivators, you will begin to establish the trust needed to assist them in addressing their core challenges.

Desperation might not repel your friends and family, but it's certainly not going to win over any large corporations. If you feel a prospective customer hesitating, make sure you're the first to say, "I can see this might not be for you right now. Can I get back to you another time later in the future?" It'll earn you respect and they'll be sure to remember you next time. Be prepared for a few "no's" along the way, respect the people who are giving them to you, and move on. There's nothing worse than moving through the sales cycle, preparing like crazy and refining proposals, only to have the prospect say "no" at the end, but while no-one likes rejection, it's part of life and it's part of learning.

3. **Listen more**

Research indicates that top-performing salespeople spend approximately 46% of the time talking and 54% listening.[44]

In comparison, average salespeople spend 68% of their time talking, and the worst performing salespeople spend a whopping 72% of their time talking![45] With those statistics in mind, make sure your pitch to customers isn't a monologue but rather a two-way dialogue. Allow them to ask questions and voice their opinions. Not only will you get time to answer, but the process will provide some really great customer insights that might help you refine your product or service offering.

Holding your opinions until the end of a meeting is a skill. Listen to understand the position that your customer is speaking from and why they have the opinions they have, and not just to hear what they say. Listen to the needs, wants and objections of your new customer. The benefits of being the last to speak means that it gives everyone else the feeling that they have been heard and contributed, while giving you the benefit of hearing what everyone else thinks before you render your opinion. Believe that you have an amazing product and are going to add value to their lives. Have on hand a list of questions to ask that will elicit more than a "yes" or "no" answer. You could start with background questions about the business as these put everyone at ease. Be sure that you are speaking to and working with the decision-makers of the company. Examples of questions could be:

- What problems are you facing?
- What are your expectations?
- What is your budget?
- When do you want to get started?
- What would you view as success?
- What is the next step?
- What else can I do to help?

Practice being the last to speak. Only once you have established a rapport is it time to paint a picture of what positive outcomes could occur if they were to implement your solution to their challenges.

4.   Connect with the decision makers

Identify upfront who it is that makes the purchasing decisions and prioritise speaking to them. In a start-up time is your greatest enemy, so it's important that you don't waste precious moments talking to the wrong people. Your presentation should offer a summary of key points that explains the benefits of your product or service.   You should provide facts that can help the person decide whether to become your business' customer. Give them tips and share your knowledge. People buy benefits, not features; they don't care about lists of ingredients as much as they care about the benefits those ingredients will deliver.

Answer your new customer's question, "What's in it for me?"

People start to own a product when they hold it in their hands, take it for a test drive, carry it into a fitting room, or in some other way get involved in a tactile manner. Make every effort to keep the conversation going by addressing any queries and objections your client may have. When your new client follows with his or her own questions or concerns, try to find out more, paraphrase to show you understand, and then present a positive response. Mirroring or repeating what your client has expressed shows that you have heard what they have said and that you understand exactly what they need. Be aware that 50% of what is said is relevant and the other 50% is body language. Fidgeting is usually a sign of stress.

5.   Close the deal

It is now decision time. Closing is a process which always ends with your customer's agreement to take action. At the conclusion of *every* interaction with your customer, ask for an agreement on the action he or she will take. Keep in mind that closing is an agreement for action on the part of your customer, and make it your goal to close every interaction. Once you have negotiated and presented your product, service or idea to your client, it's time to close the deal. It's a good idea to remain seated, have a proposal in writing on hand and make eye contact, as this shows you are interested in them and have confidence in yourself and your product or service.

There is a great "three yes" system: Ask three questions that will yield a positive response, e.g. Have we met all your criteria? Are you happy with the budget? Can we start on Monday? Once they have said "yes" three times they will be in a positive frame of mind. Hand over the proposal and a pen and don't say another word. Wait patiently for their signature and commitment. People don't believe what they hear, they believe what they see. This is the beginning of building your relationship with them and is when the real work begins.

6. Evaluate

Knowing what works and what doesn't work gives you the opportunity to re-think your process. Adjust or get rid of what doesn't work, and keep what does. If you hit your numbers, celebrate! Then look ahead to the next month. What's the goal? What's the plan? If you didn't hit your numbers, determine what might need to be changed – and change it. Then add the missed amount to the coming month's goal. You don't want to give up on the overall goal by letting the past month drop. This is a process that will work over and over again. You'll find that the momentum builds with each step, so it becomes easier and the results improve. Keep analysing and as you move forward with your plan, monitor how well it is working. On the first day of each month, take a look back at the previous month. Building your database is imperative to the growth and success of your business. Ask yourself these questions:

- How did it go?
- What worked?
- What didn't work?
- Did I hit my numbers?

Implementing a sales strategy keeps you focused and increases your chances of success. Be persistent by staying connected and building relationships with the clients you have identified. Help them help you.

According to the National Sales Executive Association in the US:[46]

- 2% of sales are made on first contact;

- 3% of sales are made on second contact;

- 5% of sales are made on third contact;

- 10% of sales are made on fourth contact; and

- 80% of sales are made on the fifth to twelfth contact!

More effective selling, essentially, is not about your product – it's about what the purchase means to your customer. You are focused on building the relationship with your client. If you understand that, you can tailor your offering to that meaning. Understanding the value of your product to the buyer also means that you can create an experience that makes them come back to you – and possibly pay a premium for it.

Making a sale is as much – if not more – about the experience and what the product or service *represents* as it is about what you're actually selling. For example, the cool factor of having an Apple product means that the average computer user is made to feel innovative and tech savvy. If you drive a BMW, what better way to reflect success than driving a premium motor car. McDonalds doesn't promise healthy eating, but that you'll love the taste and the convenience. These businesses sell the experience. Larock Fraser is an entrepreneur and writer from British Columbia, who spends his time assisting business start-ups and focuses on customer discovery and business development. He explains that, "Products are 25% of what you sell. The rest is an intangible feeling".[47]

This is a simple but powerful sales activity that can help you show the value of your product/service to a customer requesting a discount or comparing your product/service to a lower priced competitor.

Pick a participant and hold out two objects (e.g. a pen). Offer to sell him one for R100 and one for R1. Ask him which one he would like. (He will pick the R1 pen.)

Before you give it to him, explain a few things about the R100 pen: it's guaranteed for life. Even if you lose it, you can come back and get another one.

Do you still want the R1 pen?

If you show your pen at a petrol station or movie theatre, you will automatically go to the front of the line – for as long as you own the pen.

Do you still want the R1 pen?

The R1 pen will run out of ink in a week.

Do you still want the R1 pen?

The R100 pen retains 75% of its value – so you can sell it to someone else later on for R75.

Do you still want the R1 pen?

The point is that eventually, someone will pay R100 for a pen, proving that it is value, not price that drives decision-making.

7.   Hone your negotiating skills

If you are an entrepreneur, it's a given that you will have to negotiate –
and often. It can be daunting, sitting down with a client to map out the
intricacies of a major business deal, so being prepared is essential. It's also
important to try and understand both sides of the table and always consider:
under what circumstances would your client be willing to negotiate? The
secret of negotiating is to stay in control and never undervalue yourself or
your product. When you are negotiating it is important to separate your
feelings from your behaviour. It's about the best outcome for your business
and an acceptable outcome for your customer. People value things and get
greater satisfaction if they are made to work for something. If you, then I.

If you are a **poor** negotiator, you'll **spend** a fortune.
If you are a **good** negotiator, you'll **save** a fortune.
If you are a **great** negotiator, you'll **make** a fortune.

There are some misconceptions about negotiation. Here are some practical
scenarios that could help you communicate what needs to be done and turn
you into a fearless, agile and creative negotiator.

*   *When negotiating, you should ask for twice the amount you need.*

FALSE – you will end up having to climb down (and that's if they haven't
slammed the door in your face) and you will have lost an opportunity to
influence the negotiation. Go in with the intention to get to the highest
defendable position and, if you have to, move in small instalments and get
something back in return. Always trade.

*   *In a negotiation, your aim should be to prevent the other party from saying,
    "No".*

FALSE – you want to begin with a "No". If it's an immediate "Yes", you will
have lost the opportunity to negotiate.

If they agree with you immediately, you've probably done one or more of the following:

1. Made incorrect assumptions about the power balance.
2. Not identified your source of power or the weight the client has.
3. Misread how much they need or want what you have to offer.
4. Simply not asked for enough.

"No" shouldn't worry you. In fact, you should anticipate it.

- *A small concession from you to the other side will often relieve the pressure in negotiations and create goodwill.*

FALSE – they will think you are weakening and put even more pressure on you. There is a misplaced belief among many negotiators that goodwill begets gratitude – it doesn't! Goodwill actually begets greed. It reinforces the other party's competitive behaviour and encourages them to escalate it. If you make concessions without getting anything in return, the wolves will pursue you for more.

- *When negotiating, it is usually best to ask the other side to make the first proposal.*

FALSE – it's much better to take control of the process and be the one making the proposals. As long as your proposal is realistic and credible, you can use this to drive the process forward. If the other side makes the first proposal and they are unrealistic or you are not willing to meet them, then you will have an additional problem as nobody likes to be seen as backing down.

- *If you have a complaint (something you have bought has proved to be faulty or not what was promised) you should ask the supplier what they are going to do about your problem.*

FALSE – if you ask them what they're going to do to put things right, there is a chance that they will offer or give you less than you feel you are entitled to. Be specific and improve your chances of getting what you want. As long as what you have asked for is within their authority level to concede, you will achieve far better outcomes than simply relying on "What are you going to do about it?" or "Make me an offer".

You will close more deals if you maintain a can-do attitude, smile and get your client to lighten up and laugh.

Negativity always succumbs to positivity.

We love this sales story and thought it would put a smile on your face.

"Dude, you should go fishing."

A young guy from North Dakota moves to Florida and goes to a big "everything under one roof" department store looking for a job.

The Manager says, "Do you have any sales experience?" The kid says, "Yeah. I was a vacuum salesman back in North Dakota".

Well, the boss is unsure, but he likes the kid and figures he'll give him a shot. "You start tomorrow. I'll come down after we close and see how you did."

His first day on the job is rough, but he gets through it. After the store is locked up, the boss comes down to the sales floor.

"How many customers bought something from you today?" The kid frowns and looks at the floor and mutters, "One". The boss says, "Just one?! Our sales people average sales to 20 to 30 customers a day. That will have to change, and soon, if you'd like to continue your employment here".

The kid takes his beating, but continues to look at his shoes, so the boss feels bad for chewing him out on his first day. He asks (semi-sarcastically), "So, how much was your one sale for?"

The kid looks up at his boss and says, "$101,237.65".

The boss is astonished. "$101,237.65?! What the heck did you sell?"

The kid says, "Well, first, I sold him some new fish hooks. Then I sold him a new fishing rod to go with his new hooks. Then I asked him where he was going fishing and he said down the coast, so I told him he was going to need a boat, so we went down to the boat department and I sold him a twin engine Chris Craft. Then he said he didn't think his Honda Civic would pull it, so I took him down to the automotive department and sold him that 4x4 Expedition".

The boss says, "A guy came in here to buy a fish hook and you sold him a boat and a truck?"

The kid says, "No, the guy came in here to buy tampons for his wife, and I said, 'Dude, your weekend's shot, you should go fishing'".

Some of the best sales strategies are those that are built around providing genuine support and help for customers. From prospecting leads to cashing in the sales 'cheque', it's critical that you make time to educate customers, research their challenge and position yourself as a pro-active problem solver. Obviously you don't want to throw your sales goals out the window in an attempt to bend over backwards for a client, but if your primary goal is to help your prospective customer, then you're more likely to lead them to the best solution for their business.

Chapter 4

Cash in on your passion:
make money doing what you love

Intention: *to remain humble*

Affirmation: *I'm loving and loveable*

Finances

Money is energy. Ask any successful entrepreneur and they will tell you that making money is as much – if not more – about your state of mind as it is about a solid marketing plan and hard work. We like to think of business as a game and money is how you keep score. Imagine if the Springboks ran onto the field to play a rugby game against the All Blacks and there was no scoreboard! This would never have any appeal.

> *"You must gain control over your money or the lack of it will forever control you."*
>
> Dave Ramsey[48]

As entrepreneurs we tend to be jacks of all trades. We are responsible for all aspects of the business, including the finances, which may not be our area of expertise and hence something we tend to avoid. While we may be able to wing it when it comes to creative things like branding and marketing, it's not wise to do the same with the trickier financial side of the business. Finances aren't nearly as glamorous and exciting as developing an exciting marketing plan or product development, but they are essential! There are certainly no shortages of great business opportunities and ideas available today. And, whilst we often see some incredible start-ups entering the entrepreneurial arena, there is always one single glaringly obvious challenge that they all seem opposed to – financial management.

Failure to get to grips with even the most basic financial management can have a negative impact on your long-term financial strategy as well as your ability to negotiate and set up basic cost structures within the company. When you start your business, you need to know where every single cent is coming from and where it is going to. If you don't know where your money goes or how you spend it, you won't know what habits you can change in order to make your money work for you. Even your small daily expenses can make you blow your budget. Those who become millionaires are aware of the money they make and spend. True wealth is built when you spend less than you make, but to do that you need to know what you are spending. If you want to build wealth, then you need to stop wasting money. Breaking up your big financial goal into smaller tasks and keeping things simple and costs low will help you stay focused.

Let's take a look at these seven fundamentals of finance.

1. Financial management

Having a sound financial management system means keeping a set of books for your business from day one. Regardless of whether you received funds from friends, family or venture capitalists, you need to know how much of that cash has been used to set up the operations of the business. The benefits of having rigorous financial management systems are that you can:

- manage proactively rather than reactively;

- plan ahead for financing needs;

- provide financial planning information for potential investors or bank loans;

- make your business processes more efficient and hopefully more profitable;

- set growth-oriented sales goals;

- perform tax planning;

- price your services more effectively and thereby improve your gross profit margin; and

- perform a sensitivity analysis with the different financial variables involved.

Before we get into the detail, it is important to have a clear understanding of a few essential financial terms:

Bottom line

Net earnings and net income both fall under the "bottom line" description. Any action that may increase or decrease a company's net earnings or overall profit is termed the "bottom line". It's also a reference to the location of the number on a company's income statement (below both revenues – top line – and expenses).

Gross margin

Expressed as a percentage, gross margin refers to the total sales revenue that a company keeps after deducting the cost of producing its goods or services. The higher the percentage, the more the company keeps on each monetary value of sales. For example, if a company's gross margins are 25%, for every Rand of revenue that is generated, the company will retain R0.25 before paying its overheads such as salaries, rent, etc.

Fixed versus variable costs

A fixed cost is a cost that does not change with increases or decreases in the volume of goods or services that are produced by your company. These are by far the easiest to predict and plan for, and include rent, salaries and any other utilities.

Variable costs are the opposite and are dependent on the type of business you're running. Variable costs are a lot more difficult to forecast.

Equity versus debt

Equity refers to money obtained from investors in exchange for ownership of a company. Debt comes in the form of loans from banks and needs to be repaid over time. Equity and debt are equally necessary for business growth, the only caveat being that investors are not always too keen to invest in a business with too much debt. Before starting out on your entrepreneurial venture, decide whether you'd be happy to enter into an equity or debt agreement – the future of your business might rest on this!

Leverage

From a financial standpoint, leverage denotes an amount of debt that can be used to finance a company's assets. As an entrepreneur, you'll want to strike a very clear balance between your debt and equity. For example, if you have more debt than equity, you'll be viewed as "highly leveraged", which is also known as "very risky" to potential investors.

Capital expenditures (CapEx)

CapEx refers to any items purchased by your business that create future benefits. If you purchased something beneficial for your business beyond the taxable year in which you bought it, you can capitalise the items as assets in your accounting. Some examples of these items might include computer equipment, property and transportation.

Concentration

Concentration is usually defined as a percentage and measures how much business you're going to do with a specific client or partner. If you rely on one or a couple of clients and partners to do business with, this is an example of over-concentration. If something goes wrong with these limited relationships, then your business could be in serious trouble.

When it comes to finances it's always best to be proactive, which is why you need to generate financial statements on a monthly basis. These financial statements need to include:

An income statement

Otherwise known as a P&L (profit and loss statement), an income statement shows the company's revenues and expenses during a particular period and shows how the revenues are transformed into the net income. The main components of the income statement are revenues, expenses, gains and losses.

A balance sheet

This refers to a financial statement of company assets, liabilities, equity capital, total debt, etc. Whilst a balance sheet can coincide with any date, it is usually prepared at the end of a reporting period (month, quarter or year-end). The balance sheet is organised into three parts:

- Assets.
- Liabilities.
- Stockholders'/owner's equity.

A cash flow statement

A cash flow statement refers to the net amount of cash and cash equivalents that are being transferred into and out of a business. A company's ability to create value for shareholders is determined by its ability to generate positive cash flows.

The key elements of a cash flow statement are that it:

- identifies sources and uses of cash;
- tracks cash in and out at a time of movement;
- looks forward to what will happen; and
- ignores "non-cash" items.

Don't forget – Cash is King!

If you want to be a millionaire you need to understand your magic number: How much do you need to be earning an hour in order to have your dreams come true?

How do you spend your time and energy? What are your goals? Are these aligned? Look at the things you do on a daily basis; your common tasks versus your dreams or your goals. Does this everyday stuff support your big dream? It's important to understand what your time is worth.

Did you know that about 80 trillion dollars flows through the world every year?[49]

This is approximately 220 billion dollars a day. What are you doing to attract some of this?

R521 an hour x 40 hours a week x 48 weeks = R1,000,320 a year

> Dr Peter H. Diamandis is quoted as saying: "*If you want to be a billionaire, help a billion people.*"[50]

2. Revenue streams

Cash flow should be your ultimate financial priority in your business. Managing your cash is vital to ensure that all your bills are paid on time – just because your business is profitable, doesn't mean you're in the clear. A good place to start is a weekly, monthly and quarterly cash flow forecast. You need to keep track of money coming in and money going out. Dedicate at least one person to actively manage your cash flow and think critically about your on-hand cash before making any major financial decisions. Put into practice routines that help you stay cash positive, for example, you can delay payments on bills to the last possible day, and run credit checks on your customers to avoid non-payment issues. Having a good budget that is adaptable but also sets limits on your spending is a good idea. In order to make a profit, you need to have some understanding of your business finances so that you can:

- make predictions about the future;

- attract customers and deliver goods and services on a larger scale; and

- measure your progress and change direction if necessary.

There are numerous financial management tools available to help you keep accurate financial records, plan ahead for a future expense, and make sure you maximise your business' profitability.

Below are some tools that we've curated for you:

Bookkeeping: WAVE or Quickbooks

Both Wave and Quickbooks will help you to track transactions, create estimates, generate receipts, and even manage your payroll.

Forecasting: PlanGuru

Forecasting plays a huge role in how you sell your business to investors and will impact the way you strategise your spending and liquidity requirements. PlanGuru helps to model revenue and expenses and automatically generates key financial ratios and break-even analyses.

Filing: A shoebox or FileThis

Yes, some people use a shoe box to store their receipts and other such files, but it's not really recommended. A great alternative to this is a paperless document storage programme called FileThis. FileThis automatically collects and organises bills, tax receipts and any other financial documentation you might need to have stored.

3. Cost structure

Let's look at the pricing of your product or service. Are you a volume-based business or are you a value-based business? Do you want 100 clients or just 10? A volume-based business is one where you have a lot more clients and therefore need a bigger staff to support these clients, more marketing and a bigger infrastructure. A value-based business, on the other hand, means you have fewer clients but higher fees, fewer resources (e.g. staff and infrastructure) and lower costs. The approach you take will determine how you structure your pricing. There is a difference between the cost of your product, which is a science, and the price of your product, which is an art. Depending on what your product is, costing includes things like transport, storage, manufacturing, insurance, etc., whereas pricing is what you mark your product at – there isn't one correct price.

There is often a delicate trade-off between selling at a high price to improve your margin and selling at a low price to improve your volume. Your competitive edge as a small business lies in your quality, service and flexibility, so don't compromise on these. Take into account that the location of your business and the availability of your product are vitally important – people will pay more for convenience. Pricing below your competition doesn't automatically mean increased sales – you will have to have negotiated well with your suppliers and have a good marketing strategy. Pricing above your competition generally indicates high quality exclusivity that usually isn't available at another location.

Psychological pricing is pricing that customers perceive to be fair. A common method is odd pricing, using amounts that end in 5 or 9. It is believed that customers tend to round the price of R9.95 down to R9 rather than up to R10.

4. Bootstrapping

You could consider saving smartly in your business, which is building your business out of minimal resources – financial and otherwise. Bootstrapping is about managing your cash flow, making sure that the money comes in as evenly as possible, and that as little as possible goes out.

Here are some ideas on how you could bootstrap your business:

- Low upfront capital requirements – keep your running costs as low as possible, for example work from home so you don't have to pay office rent.

- Short (under a month) sales cycles – you don't want to have to wait too long for money to come in.

- Short (under a month) payment terms – when you issue your invoices, make sure they state that payment is due within a reasonably short period.

- Recurring revenue – find a way to get customers to subscribe to your product or service on an ongoing basis.

- Word of mouth advertising – if you can get customers telling their family and friends about your product or service, you can save on marketing costs.

You should use a good savings vehicle such as a money market or unit trust account and invest with the minimum allowable amount. This money will take time to grow, but if you don't touch it you won't have to get into debt in a time of crisis. If you save and invest your money by having a monthly automatic transfer, starting with a small percentage of your savings, you won't have to rely on making choices over and over again. Once you've started this habit, the opportunity to watch your balance grow will become an addiction. This long term investing will improve your quality of life experiences by reducing your debt. Head down to your local bank and get set up with a bank account. This way you'll be able to keep all your business expenses separate from your personal expenses.

There is a link between risk and reward. The greater the risk you take, the higher the potential for return. Warren Buffet is an American businessman, investor and philanthropist. He is considered by some to be one of the most successful investors in the world, and as of October 2017 was the second wealthiest person in the United States and the fourth wealthiest in the world, with a total net worth of $81.5 billion. He once said that he made his first investment at age 11 and he wondered why he waited so long.[51] If you know why money is important to you, you will be clear about what your financial planning decisions should be as you move forward in your business.

5. Danger zone

If you find yourself heading for the danger zone where your resources are depleted and you have little back-up, here are a few tips on how to avoid this at all costs:

- Don't buy the most expensive car you can afford.

- Don't apply for all the credit facilities offered to you – they could lead to overspending.

- Don't go on a spending spree at the end of every month with your new financial freedom.

- Don't put off starting to save and invest – this will create a bad habit and it becomes more and more difficult as time goes on.

- Make sound financial decisions about liabilities. Most people will have to buy their first vehicle or property with a loan from the bank.

- Don't accept the first offer from financial service providers. Get expert advice to assist you with finding the best deal that suits your lifestyle and expectations.

6. Crisis management

What happens when all hell breaks loose? Managing a crisis situation will include effective communication and patience. All management should keep in touch with employees, external clients and stakeholders. It will be very important that you train and involve several people regarding how you plan to handle each crisis situation, and ensure all information about your plan is accessible. Here are some scenarios that could potentially occur:

- Your biggest client misses a payment or closes down? Your cash flow is shot. All your future forecasts are affected.

- You experience technological failure, problems with the internet, corruption in the software, errors in passwords.

- Employees do not agree with each other and fight amongst themselves. This could result in a strike.

- Violence and theft in the workplace result in organisational crisis.

- Illegal behaviours such as accepting bribes, fraud and data or information tampering.
- Failure to pay creditors and declaring yourself bankrupt.

It will be important to keep your team's minds innovative by practicing different scenarios that could potentially occur in any one of these crisis situations. Test your plan; it will prove whether your recovery procedures are correct (or not!), and it makes people familiar with the procedures so they can function effectively in a crisis situation.

7. **Abundance mentality**

If your beliefs about money are not serving you well, change them. Create an attitude of abundance. The sayings you've grown up hearing, like: "Money is the root of all evil"[52] is not true and can contribute to limiting beliefs about money. Simply put, the overriding factor for success is our attitude and our thoughts about wealth, abundance and money. Sitting on your couch wishing you were rich won't get you far. But setting clear goals, deciding what steps you need to take to reach that goal, and approaching each step with a positive conviction that you *will* succeed – well that just might take you all the way. People are inclined to adopt the principle of 'have – do – be'. If I **have** this car/money/outfit then I will **do** this exercise/meeting/task, and I will **be** happy/successful/healthy. However, there is another way of looking at growth and development. Well known business authors, Stephen Covey, Zig Ziglar and Robert Kiyosaki discussed this principle and suggested that we rather 'be – do – have'. If I live my life by **be**ing the person I want to be, then I will **do** the things I need and I will **have** the life I choose.[53]

You don't get wealthy by working hard (only), you get wealthy by doing the right things. And it all starts with adopting the right mindset towards money. One part of it is to look for the smart way to get wealthy. Not in the sense of looking for a quick fix or doing questionable things, but by understanding what leads to wealth. This means understanding how you can create real and lasting value for others and then offering it for a good price. This is true whether you are a business-owner, self-employed or employed. If you want to be wealthy, it's time to invite it into your life. Surround yourself with people who have an abundance mentality. Learn how to become rich by reading, attending seminars and lectures, and find a way to be in the company of people who are already wealthy so that you can learn to think like them, because rich people think differently about money, wealth, themselves, other people and life.

Remember the story of Jim Carrey and the $10 million cheque he wrote himself? Being able to visualise the kind of wealth and lifestyle you would like to have is a very powerful tool. Ask yourself: What does financial success look like to me? How do I spend my time? How do I spend my energy? Do these two support each other?

Once you have the right mindset (something you might have to reinforce for yourself each day), getting your financial ducks in a row is important. Successful start-up founders are often hailed as superhuman, but the reality is they're regular people like you and I. Well, maybe not exactly like you and I! Given the unusual lifestyle of an entrepreneur, and that so many are fuelled by the promise of wild riches, it comes as no surprise that many start-up founders share inspiring stories about overcoming adversity. Here are some inspirational stories of young Africans who are making money doing what they love.

• Africa has a wealth of natural resources that are the envy of the world, one of them being cacao beans, but this lucrative global industry has been dominated for centuries by the Swiss and the Belgians. Inventive and creative South African chocolate maker, Nontwenhle Mchunu, is changing that. Mchunu started a very small home-based business in KwaZulu Natal. "The name of the business honours my cultural heritage", she explains. She is a descendent of Ezulwini Prince Dabulamanzi kaMpande's main royal house. The word "Ezulwini" means "heaven". In her business, EzulwiniChocolat, Mchunu brings together the rich history of fine chocolate making with the heritage of craftsmanship, which, she says, is the secret to her success. "I am passionate about food and craft", Mchunu says. "Chocolate proved to be the best way to combine the two things that I love most."[54]

- Another fine craftswoman is Molemo Kgomo. She couldn't find an African doll for her daughter, so she decided to create one. She now owns a company, Ntombenhle Dolls, which has grown into an entrepreneurial success. She was solving her own need and now has a full-time business to boast about.[55]

- Repurpose Schoolbags is a business that was created by two high schoolers, Thato Kgatlhanye and Rea Ngwane, who transformed discarded plastic into schoolbags. These schoolbags are functional and reduce litter in their area. It also includes a solar panel and a light, so children can see to do their homework. This business became a sustainable social enterprise that benefits school children, employs members of the community, and turns a profit.[56]

- Silulo Ulutho flipped South Africa's shortage of education into an opportunity and started offering access to computers, as well as training sessions for those who didn't know how to use a computer. Now the business has branches all over the country and is still growing.[57]

- Jacky Goliath and Elton Jeft were growing and selling fynbos and indigenous plants on the side while finishing their degrees. The demand for their plants grew and it paid more than their day jobs, which made them decide to turn their side-hustle into a full-time business, creating De Fynne nursery. They are now on a 22-hectare property with well-over 600,000 plants and 22 permanent staff to brag about. The company also supplies Woolworths, Massmart and Spar, as well as landscapers, commercial farmers and wine estates.[58]

- Christine Buchanan and her sister, Louiza Rademan, concocted their own nappy rash balm for Buchanan's first child and it worked wonders. They started out selling their product at a trade show and sold out 100 tubs on the first day. They went home, made another 100 tubs for the second and third days, and sold out on those two days as well. Now their products are sold internationally and they were able to leave their senior positions to follow their dreams.[59]

- Born in Kenya, Wangari Maathai is a passionate environmental activist who was awarded a Nobel Peace Prize for her tree-planting scheme, The Green Belt Movement. What began as a few women planting trees became a network of 600 community groups that care for 6,000 tree nurseries, which are often supervised by disabled and mentally ill people in the villages. By 2004, more than 30 million trees had been planted and the movement had branches in 30 countries. In Kenya, it has become an unofficial agricultural advice service, a community regeneration project, and a job-creation plan all in one.[60]

There's no wrong way to go about starting a business as long as you follow your heart, use your common sense, and manage your stress in a healthy way. After all, it's going to take a superhuman effort and, without a doubt, you want your business to make money. While it is essential that you get the everyday, nitty gritty financials on track, remember – money is energy, and if you have the right mindset, you will attract the kind of wealth you desire.

Chapter 5

Think forward:
create value and thrive

Intention: *I want to be heard*

Affirmation: *I have a voice worth listening to*

Leadership

Start-ups are challenged on a daily basis to meet targets, trump the competition and improve customer satisfaction, whilst simultaneously building and nurturing a team. Value-based leadership tends to be rooted in an individual's own character and relates back to what matters most to you. It's therefore important to understand and define what truly drives you and matters most in your personal and professional life in order to lay the foundation for your leadership style.

There's a huge difference between what makes someone a boss versus what makes them a leader. While a boss manages their employees, a leader inspires their staff to innovate, think creatively, and strive for greatness. All teams will have a boss that may lead the team to success, but what every team needs is a leader to help them be significant! With leaders, mutual trust and respect are hardly ever an issue, and form the foundation upon which all of their relationships are built. But building trust takes time and conscious effort as people don't trust words, they trust actions. And it's because of this that values-based communication and action are so critical to businesses today. Some people are naturally just great leaders; it's something they were born with. For the rest of us it's something we need to work towards. The good news is that developing and cultivating a positive leadership style is possible!

According to Aristotle, probably the greatest philosopher and thinker of all time, the most important goal you could hope to accomplish in the course of your life is to become an excellent person. Your purpose should be to develop the kind of personality and character that earns you the respect, admiration and affection of the important people in your world. He noted that a simple method can help if you wish to learn a virtue later in life – simply practice the virtue in every situation where that virtue is required. In other words, if you wish to develop the quality of courage, act courageously even when you feel afraid.[61]

Courage is the willingness to confront fear, pain, danger, uncertainty, or intimidation.

When we develop courage we allow ourselves to take appropriate risks, to take initiative and to act – in short, to be a decision-maker and a responsibility-taker. Just like fear can be contagious, so can courage. When a person takes a stand on what is right, they often give permission to others to do the same. That's why leadership often begins with entrepreneurship. When we cling to what's familiar or comfortable, we tend to remove risk. Unfortunately, risk is a requirement for courage. When we risk too little and rescue too quickly, we lessen our chances to grow courage.

Some important things to remember:

- You need to accept responsibility for yourself and everything in your life and build up courage by doing the things you fear.

- You will experience crisis. Only when you come across a setback, an obstacle or a difficulty do you demonstrate the kind of person you really are. It's not what you say, wish, hope or intend that reveals your character, it's your actions, especially your actions in the face of loss, that prove your quality as a leader.

- Have integrity and honesty. Develop integrity and become a completely honest person by practicing telling the truth to yourself and others in every situation.

It's not easy to rise to a position of leadership in any organisation or in any society; the competition for leadership is fierce. People who are willing to invest their time and energy will hold on to those positions and rise to the top.

Here are seven tips to cultivating leadership:

1. Communication

To lead people you must be able to clearly receive and give messages both verbally and in writing. Leaders who are good listeners value input from their team; they recognise good ideas and see how those ideas fit into the bigger picture. Leaders who have the ability to communicate their vision and goals in an inspiring way ensure that their teams know where they're going – and want to come along for the ride. By sharing your goals with your team they will feel invested and are much more likely to work hard for you, because it will feel less like they're working *for* you, and more like they're working *with* you. You would think that the more pleasant the office environment, the happier your employees will be, and the happier your employees are, the more productive they will be. However, research has proven that the opposite is true.[62] The more productive people are, the happier/more satisfied/engaged they are. It is also interesting to note that millennials (those born between 1980 and 2000), according to Oxford Economics' *Workforce 2020*[63] – *the looming talent crisis*, value formal training and mentoring more than previous generations, and want more feedback from their managers than previous generations.

Millennials opt for different internal communication tools like live chat, project management platforms, and collaboration technology as a replacement for traditional emails. They also value open offices that better facilitate communication and encourage more in-person interactions, which leads to better problem solving, more rapid collaboration and community development. By embracing technology and deliberately seeking a work/life balance, millennials make it possible for businesses to eliminate the traditional 9-to-5 schedule.

Be authentic, create a connection and always speak directly. It's vital to be able to communicate to your team what needs to be done if you are all going to work towards the same goal. This is especially true when training and hiring new employees. Be open to discussing all aspects of your business and have a full expectation exchange. All employees need to understand what their roles and responsibilities are. Allow your new candidates time to get to understand your office, encourage them to spend time in each department in order to get the full picture of how your business runs. If you have an open-door policy, your employees will trust and depend on you, and will be more willing to work hard to reach goals.

2. Consistency

Working hard, paying attention to detail, finding solutions to complex problems and following through on the completion of tasks are all very important. Leaders who see opportunities everywhere and are willing to try new things and take calculated risks are more likely to succeed. They are also open to feedback, constantly looking for ways to improve processes and performance, both for themselves and their team. Make an effort to keep your word, bring positive energy and fresh ideas to the office every day, and show commitment to your team. Consistently leading by example is the optimal way to get the best out of your team. If you want a team of hard workers, be there working alongside them when you've got a deadline looming. They will not only respect you for it, but your actions will influence the way your team sees you. To that end, keeping the promises you make is vital if your employees are to trust and respect you. Complaining and speaking badly about clients is toxic and should be avoided at all times. If you promised an early finish on Friday, stick to it. Building strong relationships based on trust is a sure way to make sure your employees stay with you.

While it can be difficult to relinquish a certain amount of control, it's vital to delegate. By moving from control mode to trusting your team, you allow them to share the responsibility of driving your business forward.   If you try to do it all yourself, you will spread yourself too thin and the quality of the work you produce will take a dive. So how do you delegate well? By getting to know what each of your team members is good at, and what they enjoy. If you assign work this way, your employees will not only produce their best work, but they will see that you trust them and feel like they play an important role in building the business.

3. Collaboration

Human labour is the most important resource in any business. For your business to succeed, you need to be collaborating with a dedicated, driven and extraordinary staff. Once you have set a clear, compelling direction for the business, the right team can take that and run with it. Think about how responsibilities and tasks will be divided into job descriptions and then trust your team to make things happen. How many people do you need and what should their skills, experience and personal qualities be? How do you hire the people who are going to strengthen your business? As a small business, it's important to focus on hiring someone you can afford and be sure to give them guidelines and clear measurable goals. When you understand yourself better you will then hire better. Your teams' skills, experience and personal qualities should complement your strengths and weaknesses. Think of being a leader like going to the gym. If you go to the gym every day for a week you won't see any immediate results, but a daily routine of connecting with your team, getting to know each of them and caring about what is happening in their world will create an impact over time. Just like in the gym, it takes months to see the results of your hard work and persistence. Only then will your interest in your employees' world begin to translate into building a culture in your business and you will start to see results. They will care about the business, work hard and not want to leave you for something better because you have invested time and energy into building these relationships and trust has formed. This is a slow and steady process, but the confidence you build will add value to your business.

4. Hire great people

Hiring the wrong person can be a real headache – and an expensive one – so it's important to use your interview to effectively weed out the good from the bad. Do research on the candidate, ask the right questions and establish a friendly rapport. This will help you gain a clear idea of whether the person is right for the job. Study their CV before the interview.

Interviewing a potential employee can sometimes be as daunting an experience as being interviewed. Put yourself in the shoes of the people you are interviewing and think about what you would like their perception of the process to be. When it comes to making hiring decisions, include team players who are able to think differently and trust your intuition about people. Hiring the right people can be difficult, so once you have found them, do your best to keep them. What's important to employees is not necessarily what you might think. Sure, a good salary is important, but people also value a good work/life balance, opportunities to advance their careers and be leaders, flexibility in terms of working hours or working remotely, and a sense of meaning from the work that they do.

Introduction

Explain how the interview process is going to work. The more comfortable your candidates are, the better rapport you can build, and the more information you will get out of them.

Questions

Try asking three questions (you will probably ask many more than three).

- Ask the candidate to speak about something he or she did well e.g. What has been your greatest accomplishment up till now?

- Ask the candidate to think about a time when they made a mistake and how they dealt with it.

- And the last question should serve as a backup in case the candidate draws a blank on one of the other questions.

Guide your candidate's conversation to specific information you are looking for, but they should do most of the talking. After several interviews, it's easy to get candidates' experiences mixed up. Make sure you write down your observations. If possible, more than one person should interview each candidate.

How do you spot a great CV in just a few seconds?

- A covering page should show a personal statement that explains why the candidate is the best person for the job. It should also include an email address.

- Usually a CV should be no more than two pages, so on average it takes just eight seconds to look at any one. It should include only the most relevant and pertinent information. Bullet points and short sentences make it easy to read with plenty of white space around the text and between categories to make the layout easy on the eye. Consistent spacing, margins and font size are important.

- At least 80% of the candidate's experience should be relevant to the job you've posted. Typos quickly show a candidate doesn't have the best attention to detail. Scan for the keywords that match the job description and ensure that the CV aligns with the company's goals and needs.

Consider hiring interns to support your team. In doing so, you will have extra hands on board and you'll provide work experience for people who are eager to learn.

Wrap-up

Give the candidate the opportunity to ask you questions. Describe what the next steps are in the process and when you plan to follow up.

Consider adding a test

You could improve your selection process if you supplement the interview with other selection methods. This could include a personality inventory or an aptitude test; Gallup StrengthsFinder is a good one which identifies an individual's top five strengths. When businesses can get employees to use their strengths on a routine basis, let's say every day, then those employees have a more direct impact on the organisation's bottom line. Gallup's research has revealed that employees who routinely use their strengths on the job are:

- 6 times more engaged;

- 7.8% more productive;

- 8.9% more profitable; and

- 3 times more likely to report a higher quality of life.

Or, have the candidate give you a presentation. Once you have narrowed your candidates down to the top three, get one of your staff members to take them to coffee and see how they get on. Ask yourself: would I work for them? Do they have integrity? Do they have the necessary skills that will add value to my business?

5. **Discipline**

Coping with stress is part and parcel of being an entrepreneur. There will be times when you have to deal with tasks that you don't enjoy and ridiculous deadlines and demands from customers. Be kind to yourself and try to maintain a positive mindset. When faced with a dispute try to respond rather than react. Learn from your mistakes and celebrate your wins. Things won't always go according to plan. When you hit a roadblock you'll have to deviate from your carefully thought-out plan, which will mean making difficult decisions, quickly.

As a leader, choosing the best from a bunch of bad options can mean asking your team for input – the most original ideas sometimes come from unlikely places (or people). It's sometimes a good idea to sleep on these big issues and take the time to think things through until the next morning; your decision could be different the following day. Don't allow fear to hold you back; instead of asking, "What if I can't do this?", rather ask, "What if I don't do this?" We are inclined to have limiting beliefs about ourselves, but by pushing ourselves outside our comfort zones and reaching our full potential, that's when the real magic happens. Your attitude plays such an important part in leadership. If you are optimistic about the future and believe in the ability of your people, this will encourage individuals to work hard and complete tasks that may otherwise have been viewed as too challenging. Being disciplined and having a positive attitude keeps group morale up, as does a sense of humour.

6. **Build a culture**

Brands all over the world have attempted to mimic "start-up culture" – a collaborative, fun and enriching atmosphere that makes employees want to come to work each day. But fostering a start-up culture is not as easy as it sounds, especially as your company grows. Having a strong culture, however, is key to success and cannot be neglected. In fact, research from the Department of Economics at the University of Warwick showed that happy employees are 12% more productive than the average worker, so it truly pays to have a strong company culture.[64]

But what exactly does a strong culture look like? And more importantly, how can you build one?

Being an effective leader is about what you do, not what you say, and a healthy company culture is evidence of a leader who understands how important this truly is to the growth of your organisation. Challenge the individuals who work in your business day in and day out to uncover new and better ways to do things. What are better methods for pleasing customers? Your employees are close to the action and are most likely to spot opportunities for innovation; often they just need some encouragement to get those ideas out in the open. People do their best work when they're passionately engaged. Passions provide us with purpose in our work, but they also give us purpose in our lives. They make us feel that we're on the right path in life and give us hope for a happy and exciting future. Cultivating an "ownership mentality" makes everyone feels like they have a stake in the company's success. Your aim should be to create a happy work environment that provides opportunities for innovation, transformation and sustainability by nurturing your staff to thrive professionally and personally. You can do this by showing appreciation; making your expectations clear; rewarding achievements, however small they may be; and by making your team feel valued. Each member of your team may appreciate different things for their personal growth and development, for example:

- interesting work;

- a high salary;

- job security;

- appreciation for work done;

- promotion within the company;

- a flexible work schedule;

- good working conditions;

- pleasant co-workers; and

- financial bonuses.

It is also up to you to foster decision-making amongst your team. By teaching them to make solid business choices, big or small, you are training your employees to be more self-sufficient and empowering them. Earn respect by listening to what your employees say, treating others with courtesy, and never committing to a promise that you can't keep. Address any issues in the office diplomatically by framing criticism in positive terms. Comment on the issue, rather than the person, for example: "I'm not sure that could work because…", or "I see some difficulties with…" In our office we have a system which we call the sh#t sandwich – start on the positive, put the criticism in the middle and close on a positive.

Let's look at two examples of companies that have succeeded at building a company culture:

Twitter employees can't stop raving about their company's culture. They have created a very team-orientated environment that encourages innovation and self-expression.[65]

It would seem wrong not to mention Google when it comes to culture. Google encourages employee risk-taking and innovation. When a vice president in charge of the company's advertising system made a mistake costing the company millions of dollars and apologised for the mistake, she was commended by Larry Page, who congratulated her for making the mistake and noting that he would rather run a company where they are moving quickly and doing too much, as opposed to being too cautious and doing too little.[66]

Many companies offer perks and benefits, and while we understand that as a start-up benefits like free food, rooftop meetings and yoga classes are unrealistic and costly, ultimately, how employees are treated and what level of ownership and trust they are given will form a key part of building your company's culture. The best culture makes all employees feel safe and welcome, never excluded or uncomfortable.

7.   Trust and transparency

Start-ups always have been and always will be high-risk environments. It's for this reason that you need to be open and honest with your team when things are going well, but even more so when things are going off course. How you communicate challenges to team members as well as investors is critical for building trust and buy-in from those who support you. That doesn't mean you need to tell your staff every single tiny detail about the business, but when it comes to areas that will directly impact them and their roles, it's best to keep them informed and up-to-date about what can and can't be done to mitigate any risky situations. A business that is value-driven and places emphasis on being significant, as well as successful, is more likely to succeed in the long-run.

Chapter 6

Maximise and manifest abundance

Intention: *I have insight*

Affirmation: *I see the big picture*

Business plan

Now that you have worked through the rainbow spectrum and got to grips with each aspect of your business, it's time to construct your business plan. This plan should be a management summary that provides proof that there is a demand out there for your product or service. It should show that your management team is experienced and balanced in its composition, that the business has the potential to be a profitable enterprise for all parties, and that the risk involved is not too great. A well-written plan is great for attracting new talent as well as investors. The written record of your goals shows that you understand your business and can deliver the results you promise. It is a document that details the past, present and intended future of your company. When investors ask, "What's your business plan?", what they are really asking is, "How do you make money?" Your business plan should be an effective guide and not a hindrance.

1. How are you going to take action on your goals?

At the start of your journey you composed a business vision, which is your big dream of who you are, and a mission statement, which clearly communicates what you are trying to achieve. You also need to include what achievements or steps you have taken to give your organisation credibility and how you are managing risk and compliance.

2. How are you getting your message to market?

All your market research on your competition and your customer segmentation, as well as your product/service features and benefits, are listed here. Your marketing strategy should show your ability to retain your customers, as well as manage and develop your business effectively. Highlight the appropriate social media platforms that speak to your specific target market and whether you are collaborating with other like-minded businesses.

3. What does your sales process look like?

Your sales strategy, operations, logistics, resources, as well as your suppliers should all be highlighted in this section of your business plan. Include all areas of your business that make sure you deliver your product to the market. Mention all the various relationships that you leverage in order to grow your sales. Potential investors can then diagnose your ability to network effectively in the marketplace.

4. How are you optimising your financial performance?

What does it cost you to run your business and how much revenue do you need to make in order to make a profit? Investors will want to see evidence of the quality of your service/product and your compliance with internal and external requirements. The structure of your capital, financial projections and investment activities should be clearly stated.

5. How are you building an effective team?

Your management plan, staff responsibilities and your ability to build an effective team will be considered. You should include the recruitment of staff, highlighting the diversity and composition of your management and team, as well as acknowledge their strengths and performance.

6. How are you delivering to expectations?

Now that you have a proper plan in place, the opportunity to pitch your business to potential investors can become a reality. When potential investors look at your business plan they will assess your character and look at your commitment to your business. They will want to see that you have met all your obligations, that your cash flow projections are in order, and that you are well prepared. They will also want to see what you could potentially fall back on should all hell break loose.

To successfully deliver on what investors want, your business plan should answer four basic questions:

- How much money is needed?
- How long will the money be needed?
- What rate of return can be expected?
- What are the risks?

7. **Critical success factors**

Here are some examples of CSFs that you could include in your business plan:

- Industry leaders through innovation.
- Nationally recognised brand.
- A culture of excellence.
- Effective leadership and management.
- Retention of key staff and scarce skills.
- Financial sustainability.
- Customer retention.
- Integrated supplier network.
- Business activity leveraged through technology.

Pitching

As a start-up you'll most likely need to pitch for finance or some form of investment at some stage of your business journey. An inspiring and impactful presentation can go a long way to making you look like a confident business owner. Start-ups frequently prepare a pitch deck which communicates key elements of their business to potential investors and venture capitalists.

Before developing your pitch and your message, have a very clear understanding and insight into who your audience will be. Ask yourself:

*   Who will I be pitching to?

*   Will there be anyone else present and if so, who?

*   Will anyone be absent from the presentation and if so, who?

*   What roles do my audience members perform in the organisation I am pitching to?

*   What will the audience already know and what requires more explanation?

*   Will there be audience members present who might have conflicting goals or objections to a potential investment?

The key to a successful pitch is preparation. Know what you want, how much you want, and why you want it. Do your homework on the investor or customer. Each time you prepare to present your business plan, consider these four critical points as your message needs to achieve a result.

*   Give your audience a reason to care.

*   Give your audience a reason to believe (include your credentials here).

*   Tell them what they need to know (your proposed growth).

*   Tell them what they need to do (how much you want).

Finally, try to make your pitch no longer than ten minutes.

1. Tell a story

Selling your business idea to investors through the means of a story doesn't just make your pitch more memorable, but it builds an emotional connection and pull with your audience too. Developing your pitch so that it flows like a story and keeping to a recommended 15-20 slide limit can be challenging. Storytelling is a scientifically-proven way to capture a listener's attention and hold it.[67] Even the most data-driven investors love a good story. Address the problem your product or service solves in the marketplace. Avoid using buzzwords and tech talk when you tell your story. Instead, use real names and real customer challenges you have experienced. Keep it simple and realistic. In the end, stories are what people will remember after they've walked away from you. Facts tell, stories sell!

Traditionally the key moments in a story should be:

- The Need: The problem/challenge/burning platform; the "villain" of the story.
- The Solution: The "hero/protagonist" of the story; what will solve the problem and destroy the villain?
- The Business Plan: What will happen after the hero takes action?
- Moving Forward: Assuming the hero is triumphant, what are the next intended steps?

Be yourself – to convince a perspective investor or buyer, you must be authentic, talk from the heart, and speak passionately about your business or product/service. Try not to show your nerves – don't use notes as they will shake when you speak.

2. Address the essentials

You don't need to address every aspect of your business plan, this will make you seem anxious, tense and nervous. Relax and know that when you're giving a pitch, less is more. Prioritise the most important things you want to share and stick to those pieces. Investors will want to hear the statistics you have researched and how your business is faring in the current market – take a nice big breath before you speak. It will help you deliver a more compelling and thoughtful pitch.

3. Focus on the pitch

Show your potential investors the actual product. The truth is, investors don't really care about your product as much as they care about the money that your product will make. Business success comes down to marketing. If you have a marketing idea, method, technique or process, this is your chance to showcase it. To be persuaded, investors have to see an airtight strategy for getting the product to market. Your business model tells an investor how your idea will (or does) convert into being economically viable.

Your business model should answer these questions:

*   What do you sell?

*   To whom?

*   How much do they pay?

*   How do they pay you?

Be concise, lucid and clear. Avoid asking questions until the end as this may distract you from your purpose, detract from the power of your pitch, or lead to something you aren't prepared for. In the preparation phase, find out as much information as possible.

4. Explain your revenue model

Investors want to make a return on their investments. They will care about your pitch if you can answer this question: *How will your company make me rich?* The answer, in investor-speak, is your revenue model and how you intend to apply it. Know your numbers – 40% of the pitch will be around numbers. (This applies to customers too.) Know the maths behind the valuation of your business or how much you need and what you need it for – be specific. Review the following before pitching to them:

External funding

- Financial institutions
- Venture capital
- Investors
- Sweat equity partnerships
- Angel funding
- Crowd funding

Offering equity

- Don't give away too much equity until you've exhausted all avenues; new entrepreneurs are often eager to get cash in return for equity. The pitfall is that when the business grows you have to give away a percentage of the equity by paying dividends. Also, an investor's involvement in the business can be stifling to an entrepreneur. Investors sometimes don't add value and unless their vision is aligned with the entrepreneur's, it's a recipe for disaster.

- Many investors will loan money to a small business but will add large amounts of interest or require a percentage of profits in addition to paying back the loan.

Doing it the hard way – funding YOURSELF

- This requires getting your hands dirty, going out and gaining new contracts or customers, and securing tenders/orders to keep the boat afloat. This is hard work but it's the best way to avoid giving equity, paying off loans with high interest, or paying annual dividends.

Net Profit

The first thing an investor wants to know is "Are you making money?" They'll review whether you have profits and losses and judge your business accordingly.

Remember, having unsustainable profits can be viewed as a negative, whilst having losses that can be improved if you're on track to scaling might be seen as a positive. Net profit refers to the amount of money that is left after you subtract your total business expenses from your total revenue.

Margins

Sales are worthless if you aren't making money. Investors will want to see your overall profit margins as well as your profit margins at an individual product level. Higher margins tend to lead to a better return for investors. Having low-profit margins means you'll need to prepare a plan that demonstrates just how you intend to improve on them. As an early-stage entrepreneur, we suggest you demonstrate how economies of scale will reduce your costs as you grow.

Cash Flow

We've touched on this before, but the fact remains that cash really is king. Cash in the bank is a sign that, as a start-up, you can deal with unexpected problems and have the necessary financial assets to capitalise on new opportunities. A sure sign of a sustainable business is free cash flow, i.e. the amount of cash that's left after you meet your expenses each period.

Debt

Debt tends to scare investors for two main reasons:

- Debt payments eat up a business' cash and high debt payments can hinder your ability to meet payroll and other necessary expenses during slow periods.

- If you go out of business, debt holders will get their money back before equity holders can claim what's left.

A simple way to measure debt is using a debt ratio. A debt ratio is a financial ratio that measures the extent of a company's leverage. To calculate this ratio you need to look at your current assets (excluding your inventory) divided by current liabilities. A quick ratio of 1 denotes that you can just meet your obligations. The higher the ratio, the more flexibility you have.

Accounts Receivable Turnover

Investors want to know how long it takes for you to collect money from customers. It tells investors two important things – if you're willing to do what's necessary to make sure you get paid, and how stable your customers are. Too often people feel awkward or even guilty for asking to be paid. As a start-up business, you can't afford to ignore non-payments. In terms of customer stability, an investor wants some sort of indication as to what your customer turnover is and whether you have a high percentage of customer write-offs (customers who don't pay).

Break-Even Point

A Break-Even Point (BEP) indicates the sales amount (either as a unit or revenue) that is required to cover a business' total costs – both fixed and variable. Total profit at a BEP is zero. Whilst investors might be accepting of some short-term losses, they would prefer to see a profit on their return sooner rather than later.

Personal Investment

Having skin in the game is important to investors, and whilst it's admirable that you've put in some sweat equity, they want to know that you've also made a financial contribution to the business.

5. Sell the dream and the vision

Investors invest in people first, and ideas second. Share the successes and traction your team has had since you started your company. Investors want to hear about your first customers, other investments put into the company (including your own sweat equity), key media placements, signed letters of intent (LOI) to purchase/partner, product and customer milestones, key hires, etc. As the CEO of your own company, you will be expected to be the lead sales person, so show the investors that you know how to sell them on your own company.

Passion and enthusiasm won't obscure your insights, integrity and realism, it will only enhance them. By anticipating tough questions, you can demonstrate your full array of abilities and traits that investors love to see. Be prepared with an accurate forecast and know how realistically you can achieve the dream. Think Big, Start Small… a motto we've always lived and believe in.

6. Handling rejection

This is inevitable, so know how to manage your emotions during the pitch, be professional and keep calm. Failure should be viewed as an opportunity to re-group, re-invent, go back to the drawing room and amend your model or plan. Start the preparation for the next pitch straight after the rejection – don't give up! Learn Learn Learn until you Earn Earn Earn!

7. An exit strategy

To some, an exit strategy sounds negative. Actually, the best reason for an exit strategy is to plan how to optimise a good situation, rather than get out of a bad one. This allows you to run your start-up and focus your efforts on things that make your company more appealing and compelling to the short list of investors you target. Every investor wants to make a lot of money in a short amount of time.

You may have considered merging with a similar company because you have complementary skills and can save resources by combining or selling to a large company, which is an efficient and quick way for them to grow their revenue and create new products. You may have decided to offer your company's shares for sale to the public for the first time. (An IPO – initial public offering – is a way for a company to raise money for its growth and upcoming projects.) Or, finally, you may have decided that enough is enough, so you close your doors and liquidate.

Whatever exit strategies you decide to share with the investors, avoid talking endlessly about your sales revenue or valuation as this could potentially shipwreck your plan. Investors want to retire comfortably on a big yacht, not just get their money back in a little equity package.

It is interesting to note that developing economies like Brazil and India have thriving entrepreneurial communities, while in South Africa a large percentage (between 30% and 50%) of new businesses fail.[68] The three main reasons for this can be summarised as a lack of information, a lack of support and a lack of financial management skills.

According to the Global Entrepreneurship Monitor's 2011 report, South Africans aren't afraid of a challenge. Approximately 64% of South African entrepreneurs are driven by a sense of opportunity rather than necessity, and nearly 73% of South Africans believe entrepreneurship is a good career choice with high social status. The key to improving entrepreneurship is thus to improve success rates through business and entrepreneurial education.[69]

Chapter 7

Make a difference and pay it forward

Intention: *I want to share my knowledge*

Affirmation: *I have endless great ideas*

Pay it forward

To thrive in your business venture, growing is key. You can offer new products, additional features, learn from other industries, and seek new investors. These investors are looking for a proven team, proven sales and proven technology. One of the blessings and burdens of taking on outside investments is that you will have to create a board of directors and they will hold you accountable. With more money comes more responsibility.

Expanding your business is easier than you might think.

You can grow your business by:

- merging with another company;
- franchising;
- marketing through television;
- marketing through social media;
- more shareholders and partnerships;
- new alliances;
- listing your company;
- going global;
- licensing your product; and
- speaking engagements.

If you do build more partnerships and alliances, make sure you get your legal ducks in a row and get it in writing!

A great tool for expanding your business is boosting your public image through publicity (PR). This is a strategic way to communicate to your target market in a business environment. You can ask magazines to interview you and write a story about your product. You can start a blog about your business and show clients the person (or people) behind the business.

When you're thinking of expanding your business, it's important to answer this question:

Can your business run without you?

Or, more bluntly, do you own your business or does your business own you?

Financial freedom is important, but if you aren't able to establish enough of a work/life balance, is it really worth it?

How do you create a business that can run without you? Hire your successor.

This, more than anything, will allow you to grow your business beyond yourself. Some questions to ask yourself:

*   When do you want this to happen? In one year? Two? Three?

*   Who will be your successor? Will you hire someone from the outside or develop the talent from within the business?

*   What are the leadership competencies that are important to this position? Strategic thinking, risk-taking or talent management?

*   What are the technical skills that are important to this position?

Mentorship

Mentorship is important for two reasons – the first being that it is part and parcel of developing a business that can run without you. It's also important in the entrepreneurship ecosystem, which comes full circle when experienced business owners share their own business lessons with those just starting out. There are no mysteries in business, there is just information you don't know yet. Being adaptable and making changes are ongoing challenges. At this stage, you can consider yourself a rainmaker – a person whose influence can initiate progress or ensure success. You are ready to pay your knowledge and experience forward.

You can do this by helping someone else succeed. This can be immensely satisfying. Time and again mentors remark on how much they get back from working with young people. When different generations come together, their blend of skills can be very complementary. Both the mentor and the mentee need to understand the mutual benefit of working together, what they expect to accomplish, and how they will go forward.

As a mentor it is important to manage your expectations and not to compare your mentees' experience to others'. There are different ways of going about building this relationship – you could decide to have your mentee work on a project, you could arrange meetings for your mentee with other senior executives at your company, you may prefer to spend one-on-one time with your mentee, or you could open up your network and contacts to your mentee and help facilitate these new relationships. Each mentoring relationship is unique and whatever approach you take, it should be mutually beneficial.

Tips for being an effective mentor:

- Develop a rapport, get to know your mentee.

- Have fun together while you learn about your mentee's goals, aspirations and needs.

- Be positive and explore feelings about various situations.

- Listen, ask questions and reflect on problems and possible solutions.

- Be realistic about your expectations and mindful of your mentee's commitment to their own growth.

- Be open to new ideas.

Nelson Mandela once said: "*What counts in life is not the mere fact that we have lived. It is what difference we have made to the lives of others that will determine the significance of the life we lead.*"[70]

Oprah Winfrey's speech to Stanford graduates[71]

To date, the Oprah's Angel Network has raised more than $80 million to help educate and empower women and children to believe in themselves, to support people around the globe in pursuing their dreams… and to provide those who are underprivileged and underserved with the means and education to reach their potential.[72]

"The world has so many lessons to teach you. I consider the world, this Earth, to be like a school and our life the classrooms. And sometimes here in this Planet Earth School the lessons often come dressed up as detours or roadblocks. And sometimes as full-blown crises. And the secret I've learned to getting ahead, is being open to the lessons, lessons from the grandest university of all, that is, the universe itself.

"It's being able to walk through life eager and open to self-improvement and that which is going to best help you evolve, 'cause that's really why we're here, to evolve as human beings. To grow into more of ourselves, always moving to the next level of understanding, the next level of compassion and growth.

"And that is really what we're all trying to do, become more of ourselves. And I believe that there's a lesson in almost everything that you do and every experience, and getting the lesson is how you move forward. It's how you enrich your spirit. And, trust me, I know that inner wisdom is more precious than wealth. The more you spend it, the more you gain.

"So, how do I define success? Let me tell you, money's pretty nice. I'm not going to stand up here and tell you that it's not about money, 'cause money is very nice. I like money. It's good for buying things.

"But having a lot of money does not automatically make you a successful person. What you want is money and meaning. You want your work to be meaningful. Because meaning is what brings the real richness to your life. What you really want is to be surrounded by people you trust and treasure and by people who cherish you. That's when you're really rich.

"So, it's a lesson that applies to all of our lives as a whole. What matters most is what's inside. What matters most is the sense of integrity, of quality and beauty. I got that lesson. Know that your voice has power."

Sometimes rainbows inexplicably show up; they are said to represent clarity and are a source of magical energy. So look for them everywhere you go and you are more likely to attract the things you desire. No successful person, whether they are athletes, billionaires or geniuses, ever achieved success on their own. Surround yourself with people who support and believe in you and your dreams.

We trust that you are excited, equipped and ready to take the next steps on your entrepreneurial journey. And while we understand that this journey can often be a long and lonely road filled with many crossroads and important decisions, often with far reaching significance, the fact that you have taken the time to work through the colours of the rainbow shows you are committed, you are a doer and you want success. You have cultivated a passion for your business and a desire for ongoing development and we congratulate you!

We came across this beautiful story and thought it would be apt to place it here at the end of our book to remind us of the importance of finding balance in our busy lives.

Once upon a time, a very strong woodcutter asked for a job with a timber merchant. The timber merchant took one look at the woodcutter's strong shoulders and gave him the job. The woodcutter was very happy. The pay was great and the woodcutter was determined to do his best.

The timber merchant gave the woodcutter an axe and showed him the trees that needed to be felled. **On the first day, the woodcutter felled 18 large trees.**

"Congratulations", the boss said, "Nobody has ever felled 18 huge trees in one day before. I'm really impressed!"

Very motivated by the timber merchant's words, the woodcutter tried harder the next day, but he could only fell 15 trees. He was very upset with himself and his performance, so on the third day he tried even harder, but to his dismay, he could only fell 10 trees.

Day after day, even when he worked from dawn 'til dark, he was cutting down fewer and fewer trees and struggling more and more each day!

"I must be losing my strength", the woodcutter thought. He went to his boss and apologised profusely, saying that he could not understand what was going on.

"When was the last time you took some time-out to sharpen your axe?", the timber merchant asked.

"Sharpen my axe?", asked the woodcutter. "I had no time to sharpen my axe. I was too busy trying to cut down trees…!"

Sometimes we make things much harder for ourselves than they need to be. We don't take the time to sharpen our own axe. We neglect to relax our bodies… clear our minds… manage our emotions… prioritise the important things… and because of this, we feel busy and yet we accomplish less and end up stressed, overwhelmed and unhappy.

You may have been taught that success only comes from hard work. There's nothing wrong with hard work, but is working harder really the answer? Because if it were, many of us would already have all the success we ever wanted.

Remember the importance of quiet time, meditation or doing things that restore your balance.

Join our Golden Circles

Our Golden Circle programme provides a peer-to-peer learning support system. Confidentiality and commitment are two of the founding principles of these groups. Our highly skilled mentors and facilitators will guide you in identifying exciting opportunities on the horizon. We understand that business success does not lie in silos, but is rather intertwined with both family and personal commitments and obligations. We facilitate the sharing of current challenges and/or opportunities, business or personal.

In summary, our Golden Circle groups are:

- a confidential, peer-sharing programme chaired by highly skilled and professionally trained moderators;
- groups of 8-12 entrepreneurs at similar growth check-points in their journey;
- structured meetings that last for 3-4 hours (approximately 11 meetings per year); and
- based on the tenants of personal responsibility, Gestalt Mindset and confidentiality.

Golden Circle offers:

- the opportunity to take risks;
- opportunities to share information, learn, grow and support each other;
- experience sharing that spans personal and professional topics;
- opportunities to share fears and vulnerabilities; and
- the chance to help a peer make a positive change.

Sign up now at www.overtherainbow.mobi

We can't wait to welcome you!

Endnotes

1   The Global Entrepreneurship Monitor (GEM). (2017). *Global Report 2016/2017.* Retrieved from: https://www.gemconsortium.org/report/49812

2   International Labour Organization (ILO). (n.d.). *The World Bank Group and ILO Universal Social Protection Initiative.* Retrieved from: https://www.ilo.org/global/topics/social-security/WCMS_378991/lang--en/index.htm

3   Indian Legends. (n.d.). *The Legend of the Two Wolves.* Retrieved from: https://www.firstpeople.us/FP-Html-Legends/TwoWolves-Cherokee.html

4   The Global Entrepreneurship Monitor (GEM). (2017). *Global Report 2016/2017.* Retrieved from: https://www.gemconsortium.org/report/49812

5   Rubin, B.F., & Cheng, R. (2015). *Fire Phone one year later: Why Amazon's smartphone flamed out.* Retrieved from: https://www.cnet.com/news/fire-phone-one-year-later-why-amazons-smartphone-flamed-out/

6   Hessel, E. (2009). *MySpace's Yelp Envy.* Retrieved from: https://www.forbes.com/2009/03/31/myspace-yelp-facebook-technology-myspace.html#3edd4dc279b8

7   Dweck, C. (n.d.). *Carol Dweck: A Summary of The Two Mindsets And The Power of Believing That You Can Improve.* Retrieved from: https://fs.blog/2015/03/carol-dweck-mindset/

8   mPower People Solutions. (n.d.). *About Lele Mehlomakulu CDWF, Founder and MD.* Retrieved from: http://www.mpower-ps.co.za/

9   iLearn Onsite|Online|Training. (n.d.). *Our Storey.* Retrieved from: https://www.ilearn.co.za/about/our-story

10 Entrepreneur. (2017). *Nando's Adopts Technology; Focuses on Food & Funny.* Retrieved from: https://www.entrepreneurmag.co.za/advice/franchising/franchise-news/nandos-adopts-technology-focuses-on-food-funny/

11 Red & Yellow Creative School of Business. (n.d.). *Hello!.* Retrieved from: https://www.redandyellow.co.za

12 Carrol Boyes (n.d.). *Our Story.* Retrieved from: https://carrolboyes.com/za/our-story/

13 I am an entrepreneur. (n.d.). Retrieved from: https://iamanentrepreneur.co.za/

14 Entrepreneur Magazine. (2018). *30 Top Influential SA Business Leaders.* Retrieved from: https://www.entrepreneurmag.co.za/advice/success-stories/entrepreneur-profiles/30-top-influential-sa-business-leaders/27/

15 Motheo Contruction Group. (n.d.). *About us.* Retrieved from: http://www.motheogroup.co.za/about.php.

16 Albertyn, D. (2018). *Watch List: 50 Black African Women Entrepreneurs To Watch.* Retrieved from: https://www.entrepreneurmag.co.za/advice/women-entrepreneurs/women-entrepreneur-successes/watch-list-50-black-african-women-entrepreneurs-to-watch/

17 Kenny, G. (2014). *Your Company's Purpose Is Not Its Vision, Mission, or Values.* Retrieved from: https://hbr.org/2014/09/your-companys-purpose-is-not-its-vision-mission-or-values

18   Norris, E. (2017). *How did Richard Branson make his fortune?* Retrieved from: https://www. investopedia.com/ask/answers/032615/how-did-richard-branson-make-his-fortune.asp

19   Virgin Unite. (n.d.). *From The Rebel Billionaire to a $56 million IPO.* Retrieved from: https://www.virgin.com/richard-branson/rebel-billionaire-56-million-ipo

20   Branson, R. (2013). *Richard Branson on Taking Risks.* Retrieved from: https://www. entrepreneurmag.co.za/advice/business-leadership/leading/richard-branson-on-taking-risks/

21   Google. (2013). *About Google: Mission Statement.* Retrieved from: https://www.google. com/about/

22   Pioneer Foods. (n.d.). *Our Vision and Mission.* Retrieved from: http://www.pioneerfoods. co.za/about/our-vision-and-mission/

23   FlySafair. (n.d.). *Our Vision & Mission.* Retrieved from: https://www.flysafair.co.za/about-us

24   Vodacom. (n.d.). *Our mission: The Vodacom way is the only way.* Retrieved from: https:// www.vodacom.co.ls/ls-about-us/our-mission

25   GALA (Globalization & Localization Association. (n.d.). *Organization overview: Uber.* Retrieved from: https://www.gala-global.org/company-directory/uber

26   PetroSA. (n.d.). *Vision, Mission, Values.* Retrieved from: http://www.petrosa.co.za/ discover_petroSA/Pages/Vision-Mission-Purpose.aspx

27   Spar. (n.d.). *Vision.* Retrieved from: https://investor-relations.spar.co.za/ir2017/who-we-are/our-vision-purpose-values/

28   University of KZN. (n.d.). *Vision & Mission.* Retrieved from: https://www.ukzn.ac.za/ about-ukzn/vision-and-mission/

29   Barry Winbolt Personal and Professional Development. (2016). *9 Ways to Improve Your Resilience at Work.* Retrieved from: https://www.barrywinbolt.com/resilience-at-work/

30   Maddi, S.R. & Khoshaba, D.M. (1994). Hardiness and Mental Health. *Journal of Personality Assessment, 63*(2):265-74. Retrieved from: https://www.researchgate.net/ publication/15232811_Hardiness_and_Mental_Health

31   The balance small business. (2018). *SMART Goal Examples.* Retrieved from: https://www. thebalancesmb.com/smart-goal-examples-2951827

32   McCormack, M. H. (1984). *What they don't teach you at Harvard Business School.* Toronto: Bantam Books.

33   High Existence. (n.d.). *Dalai Lama's 18 Rules for Living" Expanded.* Retrieved from: https://highexistence.com/rules-for-living/

34   Entrepreneur Franchise 500. (2015). *Success Can Come at Any Age. Just Look at These 6 Successful Entrepreneurs.* Retrieved from: https://www.entrepreneur.com/article/241346

35   Wikipedia. (n.d.). *Jim Carrey.* Retrieved from: https://en.wikipedia.org/wiki/Jim_Carrey

36   Christensen, C. M. (1997). *The innovator's dilemma: when new technologies cause great firms to fail.* Boston, MA: Harvard Business School Press.

37   Nobel, C. (2011). *Clay Christensen's Milkshake Marketing.* Retrieved from: https://hbswk. hbs.edu/item/clay-christensens-milkshake-marketing

38   Structure & Narrative. (2019). *Theory of Change and The Golden Circle. – Structure & Narrative.* Retrieved from: https://sjef.nu/theory-of-change-and-the-golden-circle/.

39 BrainyQuote. (n.d.). *Meg Whitman Quotes*. Retrieved from: BrainyQuote.com Web site: https://www.brainyquote.com/quotes/meg_whitman_406473

40 Black, N. (2009). *Research + Psychology: Exploring the motivations behind human behavior*. Retrieved from: https://www.nickblack.org/

41 BrainyQuote. (n.d.). *Mark Twain Quotes*. Retrieved from: BrainyQuote.com Web site: https://www.brainyquote.com/quotes/mark_twain_414009

42 Efti, S. (n.d.). *5 mega-successful entrepreneurs who launched their careers in sales*. Retrieved from: https://blog.close.io/5-mega-successful-entrepreneurs-who-launched-their-careers-in-sales

43 Edufruit Institue Management System. (2011). *Successful Entrepreneurs Survive being told "NO"*. Retrieved from: http://edufruit.com/?p=384

44 Premer, D. (n.d.). *5 Tips for Mastering theARt of Listening in Sales*. Retrieved from: https://cerebralselling.com/mastering-sales-listening/

45 Ibid.

46 Robers, S. (2014). *Those incredible sales stats everyone cites are actually completely false*. Retrieved from: https://venturebeat.com/2014/08/15/these-incredible-sales-stats-everyone-cites-are-actually-completely-false/

47 Ibid.

48 All Author(n.d.). *Dave Ramsey Quotes*. Retrieved from: https://allauthor.com/quote/93565/

49 Hartman, M. (2017). *How much money is there in the world?* Retrieved from: https://www.marketplace.org/2017/10/30/world/how-much-money-there-world

50 Diamandis, P. (n.d.). *How to become a billionaire*. Retrieved from: https://www.diamandis.com/blog/how-to-become-a-billionaire

51 Jenkins, A. (2017). *Warren Buffett's Net Worth Has Reached a Staggering New High*. Retrieved from: http://fortune.com/2017/10/24/warren-buffett-net-worth/

52 Thum, M. (2013). *The 10 Most Limiting Beliefs about Money (& How to Remove them)*. Retrieved from: https://www.myrkothum.com/limiting-beliefs-about-money/

53 The Total Man. (n.d.). *The Be, Do and Have Principle*. Retrieved from: http://www.thetotalman.com/Newsletter-Archive/Be-Do-Have-Principle.htm

54 Abrahams, G. (2009). *Ezulwinichocolat: Nontwenhle Mchunu: A young entrepreneur from KwaZulu Natal has built her business on the art of making fine chocolate*. Retrieved from: https://www.entrepreneurmag.co.za/advice/success-stories/upstarts/nontwenhle-mchunu-heavenly-delights/

55 Verduyn, M. (2016). *Molemo Kgomo Of Ntombenhledolls Turns Business Into Child's Play*. Retrieved from: https://www.entrepreneurmag.co.za/advice/success-stories/snapshots/molemo-kgomo-of-ntombenhledolls-turns-business-into-childs-play/

56 Verduyn, M. (2015). *How the Rethaka Founders Funded Their Business By Winning Competitions*. Retrieved from: https://www.entrepreneurmag.co.za/advice/success-stories/snapshots/how-the-rethaka-founders-funded-their-business-by-winning-competitions/

57 Silulo Ulutho Technologies. (n.d.). *Welcome to Silulo Ulutho Technologies*. Retrieved from: http://silulo.com/

58   Defynne Nursery. (n.d.). *Our story*. Retrieved from: http://www.defynne.co.za/index.php/about-us/our-story

59   Crampton, N. (2018). *20 South African Side-Hustles You Can Start This Weekend*. Retrieved from: https://www.entrepreneurmag.co.za/advice/starting-a-business/types-of-businesses-to-start/20-south-african-side-hustles-you-can-start-this-weekend/21/

60   The Green Belt Movember. (n.d.). *Wangari Maathai*. Retrieved from: https://www.greenbeltmovement.org/wangari-maathai

61   Younkins, E. (2003). *Aristotle, Human Flourishing, and the Limited State*. Retrieved from: http://www.quebecoislibre.org/031122-11.htm

62   The Chief Happiness Officer Blog. (2007). *Top 10 Reasons why Happiness at Work is the Ultimate Productivity Booster*. Retrieved from: https://positivesharing.com/2007/03/top-10-reasons-why-happiness-at-work-is-the-ultimate-productivity-booster/

63   Oxford Economics. (2014). *Workforce 2020: The Looming Talent Crisis*. Retrieved from: https://www.oxfordeconomics.com/recent-releases/workforce-2020-the-looming-talent-crisis

64   Oswald, A.J., Proto, E., & Sgroi, D. (2015). *Happiness and Productivity*. Retrieved from: https://wrap.warwick.ac.uk/63228/7/WRAP_Oswald_681096.pdf.

65   Huddleston, T. (2014). *Twitter tops all in culture and values, employees say*. Retrieved from: http://fortune.com/2014/08/22/twitter-tops-list-company-culture/

66   Lashinsky, A. (2006). *Chaos by design*. Retrieved from: http://archive.fortune.com/magazines/fortune/fortune_archive/2006/10/02/8387489/index.htm

67   Patel, N. (2015). *13 Tips on How to Deliver a Pitch Investors Simply Can't Turn Down*. Retrieved from: https://www.entrepreneur.com/article/251311

68   Investopedia. (n.d.). *Top 6 Reasons New Businesses Fail*. Retrieved from: https://www.investopedia.com/slide-show/top-6-reasons-new-businesses-fail/

69   Kelly, D.J., Singer, S., & Ilerrington, M. (2011). 2011 *Global Report*. Global Entrepreneurship Monitor. Retrieved from: https://www.gemconsortium.org/report

70   Mandela, N. 2002. *Address by Nelson Mandela during the 90th birthday celebration of Mr Walter Sisulu*. Retrieved from: http://www.mandela.gov.za/mandela_speeches/2002/020518_sisulu.htm

71   Standford Report. (2008). *Oprah talks to graduates about feelings, failure and finding happiness*. Retrieved from: https://news.stanford.edu/news/2008/june18/como-061808.html

72   Anonymous. (2014). *How has Oprah Winfrey impacted the world?* Retrieved from: https://www.quora.com/How-has-Oprah-Winfrey-impacted-the-world

Index

www.ingramcontent.com/pod-product-compliance
Lightning Source LLC
Chambersburg PA
CBHW071149200326
41519CB00018B/5171